The Origins of
Family Psychotherapy

The Origins of Family Psychotherapy

The NIMH Family Study Project

Murray Bowen, MD
Edited by J. Butler, with contributions by
M. Kerr and J. Bowen

JASON ARONSON
Lanham • Boulder • New York • Toronto • Plymouth, UK

Published by Jason Aronson
A wholly owned subsidiary of The Rowman & Littlefield Publishing Group, Inc.
4501 Forbes Boulevard, Suite 200, Lanham, Maryland 20706
www.rowman.com

10 Thornbury Road, Plymouth PL6 7PP, United Kingdom

British Library Cataloguing in Publication Information Available

Library of Congress Cataloging-in-Publication Data

Bowen, Murray, 1913–1990.
  [Papers. Selections]
  The origins of family psychotherapy : the NIMH Family Study Project / edited by J.
Butler ; with contributions by M. Kerr and J. Bowen.
      pages cm
  Includes bibliographical references and index.
  ISBN 978-0-7657-0974-5 (cloth : alk. paper) — ISBN 978-0-7657-0975-2 (electronic)
1. NIMH Family Study Project (U.S.) 2. Family psychotherapy—Research—United
States. 3. Family psychotherapy—United States—History. I. Butler, J., 1945– II. Title.
  RC488.5.B673 2013
  616.89'156—dc23   2012051541

Printed in the United States of America

Contents

Foreword

*Joanne Bowen, Ph.D., Chair of the
Board & President of Leaders for Tomorrow*

I am pleased and honored to write a foreword to *The Origins of Family Psychotherapy: The NIMH Family Study Project,* an edited volume of Murray Bowen's unpublished and published papers. Written when he was a young research scientist at the National Institute of Mental Health in Bethesda, Maryland, they represent the early years of his professional odyssey toward a science of human behavior, when he observed entire families living on a research ward. The world has known more about Murray Bowen's subsequent work with families; here readers have the opportunity to read firsthand his early thinking.

I write as both Murray Bowen's daughter and President of Leaders for Tomorrow, a public charity that has dedicated itself to finding resources to contribute to making the Murray Bowen Archives, which are housed at the National Library of Medicine in Bethesda, Maryland, available to the world for research and education, and available to interested members of the public. I also want to thank John Butler, M.S.W, Ph.D., who realized the significance of these papers and began his project to publish them together along with Bowen's early published works. Together, these papers chronicle the origin of family psychotherapy, communicated in Bowen's own words.

As a young child, I understood my father, Murray Bowen, was involved in something special. Later, as a teenager, I attended local and national meetings, and here I learned the basics of what was to become known as Bowen Theory. It was a privilege to witness the important role Murray Bowen played amongst his peers and the growth of the new field of family psychotherapy that emerged. On some level, I understood the trials and tribulations of this creative scientist. However, it took reading the reports and papers in this volume for me to more

1

fully comprehend the enormity of what he accomplished during his five years at the National Institute of Mental Health (1954–1959).

Murray Bowen was a brilliant scientist, who observed life and all relationships existing between humans and their natural world. During his residency at the Menninger Clinic in Topeka, Kansas, he understood schizophrenia was a family problem, but he believed the primary relationship involved the mother and infant-child, which persisted into the child's adult life. When he began his research at NIMH, he believed the psychosis could be reversed if the mother could relinquish the child. Over the course of his first year at NIMH, however, he observed the role other family members played, and within a year incorporated entire nuclear families into the study.

Murray Bowen's path became one of an ethologist, a scientist who studies animal behavior and the social relationships that sustain life. Observing the entire family enabled him to observe the emotional intensity of the mother/child relationship as it existed in, and was influenced by, the family emotional unit.

To hear Murray Bowen tell it, he came up with this idea himself. On another level, his upbringing provided the foundation for his ethological research. He was born in Waverly, Tennessee, a small town sixty miles west of Nashville. His family owned Luff-Bowen, a business that initially sold furniture, household goods, and coffins, and later expanded to include a funeral home. His father's parents, Jess Sewell Bowen and Maggie May Luff Bowen, his uncle, Edmund J. Luff, and his four siblings lived on a nearby farm. Bowen often spoke of the importance of his childhood in this town, where everyone knew one another and their families. His father, who was a town leader, often remarked to his family that he either knew a person personally or he knew their kin by the way they walked.

On the farm where they worked the land and raised livestock to produce virtually all their food on a two-acre garden and 50-acre pasture, Murray Bowen experienced the deep connection humans have with the earth and each other. He vividly described his childhood, "As kids we worked our lives away to help Mother prepare the year's food from the fields, garden, orchards, kill farm animals, (and more) . . . A hired man butchered hogs, plowed the field with his mule, and did other odd jobs. Hired girls helped indoors. Family members planted, milked, stacked wood, made sausage and cider, and stored fruit and vegetables."

There is more—Bowen described his father's knowledge of the natural world and his effort to pass this knowledge on to his children:

> He KNEW botany and what it was about, and he could predict weather from moss on trees, the thickness of animal furs, and the density of fogs. . . . He knew each and every sound from birds and animals . . . (He) determined his

kids would know the land and he put a tremendous amount of time with his sons hunting and fishing, inspecting crops, gathering nuts, explaining his built-in knowledge of Nature.

Bowen summarized his life, "I shall always be grateful for having the parents I did and for the 'penniless' (but successful) situation in which I grew up." He understood this knowledge came from living it.

Bowen was an observer of humans and their relationships with each other. Having lived in a small rural community where families had lived for generations, he understood the important role social relationships play in sustaining the very fabric of an agricultural community. Bowen's genius was far greater—he had an intuitive understanding of the role emotions play in every relationship—within and amongst families, in communities, and in nations. He could see emotions underlying well thought-out positions, when others saw logic. He often remarked, "Humans can think about, think about, think about." To him what counted was not what humans said, but what they did, and he observed behavior as would a biologically trained ethologist. Ultimately, he developed a natural systems theory about the biological basis of human relationships.

Managing a ward of families with diagnosed schizophrenics and working with medical staff trained in individual-based therapy had to have been the ultimate challenge. I heard my father describe those days and the trials and tribulations that came with the growth in the project. Everyone engaged in the project had to have experienced challenge: the staff, who had been trained in individual psychoanalytic therapy; the administrators, as they engaged new ground rules for a therapeutic relationship; and Bowen himself, who was breaking new ground, bringing about a paradigm shift, and navigating relationships steeped in the paradigm of individual therapy. Reading the reports and papers in this volume has left me with a profound understanding of the monumental nature of his accomplishments.

The reports and papers lay out the progress of this natural experiment—and they demonstrate what it took for him to be a neutral presence in an emotional storm. I must say, I am now more than ever in awe of my father and his accomplishments.

The outcome discussed in this volume speaks for itself. Within five years, Murray Bowen had come to understand schizophrenic psychosis in a patient as a symptom of an active process involving every member of a family (Bowen, 1959, 6). The family was a unit rather than a collection of individuals, and individual behavior was viewed through the lens of the emotional *unit*. True to his training in science and medicine, Bowen collected data from the psychiatrist who also served as the families' primary care physician, evidence that allowed him to see the phenomenon of the reciprocal relationship existing between family members and their health. He was now able to hypothesize on the interaction between emotional and physical symptoms.

This shift in perspective, from individual to family unit in its physical and emotional manifestations, allowed Bowen to see broad patterns of "form and movement that had been obscured by the close-up view of the familiar individual orientation" (Bowen 1959, 10). The basics of family psychotherapy emerged, one where his staff thought about, related to, treated, and saw the family as a unit. And out of this project came the development of a set of systematic principles based on his research.

This volume of papers gives a glimpse into Bowen's odyssey towards a science of human behavior. The collection of papers and audiovisual records now housed at the National Library of Medicine chronicle his remarkable odyssey far more fully. Murray Bowen wrote tirelessly, preparing papers for professional meetings, corresponding with many family members and professionals about those meetings, and sharing new ideas and observations of current events. The inventoried manuscript collection alone includes over 150 linear feet of videos, professional and personal correspondence, NIMH records, manuscript drafts, clinical records, family histories, photographs and other documents—a virtual treasure trove.

In 2008, an informal association of volunteers, with me as chair, formed a committee to determine how to find private resources to supplement NLM's federal funding. In late 2008, Andrea Schara, founder and president of Leaders for Tomorrow, offered her organization as a home for this important work. I became the new president and executive director. Its Board of Directors reorganized to position the organization to obtain and administer resources to carry out its new vision and mission, which is to give Bowen theory to the world.

Leaders for Tomorrow's mission is to promote, support, and contribute to the preservation and processing of Murray Bowen's Archives at the National Library of Medicine; aid in the development of an internet-based search and access capability; facilitate additions to the Archives; foster scholarship using the Archives; and foster the dissemination of this scholarship.

This volume, which includes a number of reports and papers from Bowen's NIMH research, inaugurates LFT's support of scholars' research using the Murray Bowen Archives. I invite readers to explore Murray Bowen's curious mind at work, as I have done in preparing the Foreword to this volume. It has given me great satisfaction as his daughter and as LFT's President to have done so.

Joanne Bowen, Ph.D.
President, Leaders for Tomorrow

Foreword

Michael E. Kerr, M.D.

I first became aware of some of Murray Bowen's ideas about families in 1965 at a lecture he gave during my junior year at Georgetown University Medical School. I was instantly attracted to what he had to say because an older brother of mine had been diagnosed with schizophrenia three years earlier. Bowen was the first person I had heard talk about the mothers of schizophrenic people without judging them. He described their profoundly deep involvement in the lives of their son or daughter and rejected notions such as inadequate mothering or repressed hostility as the "cause" of their offspring's dysfunction. He also talked about understanding the intensity of the mother-dysfunctional offspring relationship as the outcome of a multigenerational process. Furthermore, he described how the mother-child relationship was always part of a larger nuclear family process.

My brother was diagnosed to have schizophrenia during his first psychiatric hospitalization in August 1962. My father had died suddenly just three months earlier. My brother's behavior became increasingly bizarre during the summer following Dad's death. We contacted a psychiatrist who suggested that my brother was mentally ill and recommended hospitalization. The hospitalization was a positive experience in that my brother and the rest of the family all calmed down. Years later, as I got to know more about Bowen theory and the family as an emotional unit, I could appreciate how anxious our family had gotten following Dad's death. My brother's symptoms fit the descriptive criteria of a mental illness, but I could see that it was family anxiety that drove his aberrant behavior to such an extreme. It became clear to me that my family's reactivity had presented as much a problem for my brother as my brother's aberrant behavior presented for the family. The toxic dynamic for my brother, however, was that we saw his actions as the "cause" of our reactions. Blaming my brother for the family's distress only aggravated his panic and emotional isolation.

My brother's hospitalization occurred three years after Bowen's family research project at N.I.M.H. had concluded. Had the psychiatrist we consulted understood families and helped us focus less on my brother and more on how panicked and out of control the rest of us were, the hospitalization would likely have been avoided. Psychiatric hospitalizations are sometimes necessary to avoid serious complications for the patient and the family, but many hospitalizations can be avoided by addressing the level of family anxiety rather than focusing on mental illness being the cause of the crisis situation.

The experience with my brother contributed significantly to my decision during psychiatric residency to learn and practice Bowen's theoretical framework rather than pursue an individually oriented approach. I worked closely with Bowen after my training until his death in 1990 and then succeeded him as director of the Family Center that he founded at Georgetown University in 1975.

Beyond the application of Bowen's ideas to clinical problems, *Bowen family systems theory's* conceptualization of the family as an emotional unit and its application of systems thinking to address the complex interactions in the unit are significant steps toward the development of a science of human behavior. By observing how family members interact, as Bowen and his research team did at the N.I.M.H., it was possible to describe family interactions and their impact as factually as astronomers describe the motions of the planets. Furthermore, Bowen assumed that emotional forces, a legacy of man's long evolutionary heritage, governed human family relationships and that the specific interactive patterns he had observed in human families likely operated in other species. Furthermore, subsequent outpatient family research bore out Bowen's hypothesis that the forces and patterns operating in families with schizophrenia were an exaggeration of those that play out in all families.

Bowen theory is a new theory of human behavior and, like other theories, has been vulnerable to becoming a "closed system," becoming a dogma. Bowen's approach for keeping the theory open and subject to modification based on new facts was to maintain viable contact with the accepted sciences. This effort has guided those working to continue the development of Bowen theory during the fifty plus years since the N.I.M.H. project ended. The emphasis on interdisciplinary exchange with researchers studying human beings and other forms of life continually subjects the accuracy of Bowen theory to scrutiny. Thus far, the myriad facts emerging from a wide range of disciplines have been consistent with Bowen theory. Much valuable knowledge has also been gained from decades of applying the theory in clinical, organizational, and community settings.

Murray Bowen left behind a huge archival collection of papers, letters, videotapes, and other materials. Dr. Butler has been among those with the motivation and discipline to read the original documents and learn about some of the key research observations that led to the theoretical concepts Bowen developed. I would compare his effort to someone reading Darwin's notes from his five-year voyage on the *H.M.S. Beagle.* Darwin was the first to make such a voyage of discovery and it gave him a unique perspective on the broad spectrum of living things. Bowen was the first to study whole family units on a research ward for extended periods and that gave him a unique, larger system perspective on the forces that govern human behavior. The importance of the N.I.M.H. project in powerfully shaping a new theory of human behavior, first published in 1966, makes Dr. Butler's careful study of Bowen's earliest writings especially interesting and important.

Michael E. Kerr, M.D.

Preface

This book is a collection of some of Murray Bowen M.D.'s important unpublished and published papers written during the NIMH Family Study Project from 1954 to 1959. On October 9, 2002, the Bowen family deeded the papers of Murray Bowen, M.D. to the History of Medicine Division of the National Library of Medicine. This was quite a gift. Dr. Bowen was a psychiatrist who lived from 1913 to 1990, and at the time of his death was the Director of the Georgetown Family Center in Bethesda, Maryland. This is not the first effort to publish some aspect of the Bowen archives and it will not be the last. For example, there is edited a self-published work called *Commitment to Principles: The Letters of Murray Bowen, M.D.* (Boyd, 2008).

For the past several years, in advance of the fall and spring meetings at the Bowen Center for the Study of the Family, I had the privilege of researching Bowen's papers in the History of Medicine Division, National Library of Medicine on the campus of NIMH in Bethesda, Maryland. A research proposal was submitted to the History of Medicine Division in order to obtain access to Dr. Bowen's papers. The proposal focused on a long-term review of unpublished annual summaries, project description sheets, unpublished papers, presentations, and published papers from the Family Study Project relating to the origin of family psychotherapy. Many of these documents formed the basis of Bowen's later writings that have become so familiar to many in the mental health field.

OVERVIEW

It is my hope that this publication will present some of Dr. Bowen's original writings to undergraduate and graduate students, clinicians in the various mental health fields, researchers, and serious students of Bowen family systems theory. Bowen was not the only researcher interested in studying schizophrenia. At the time of his research from 1954 to 1959, many others were studying and researching this particular clinical problem. However, Bowen was the first to hospitalize entire families containing a child diagnosed with schizophrenia. Bowen's Family Study Project has been called "The Camelot of Family Research" (Guerin, 1972).

Bowen's interest in schizophrenic patients predated his NIMH project and began during his time at Menninger's from 1946 to 1954. He became intrigued with the psychological symbiosis between these patients and their parents. It was the NIMH research that provided the time and resources for an in-depth study and research of this problem.

Initially mother-daughter dyads were admitted to a special unit on the NIMH grounds where they would live in residence. Later, when it became apparent that family members important to the mother were also involved in the problem, fathers and siblings of the patient were admitted. The average length of stay for project families was about a year, which is difficult to imagine by today's standards. Keeping families engaged for that length of time was a significant accomplishment. While Bowen (1978) published some articles about the Family Study Project in the first part of his book *Family Therapy in Clinical Practice*, the original documents in this book offer rich detail and history previously unavailable. The original papers are the first act in a two-act drama; his published papers in *Family Therapy in Clinical Practice* are act two.

SIGNIFICANCE OF THE PAPERS

One basic question is: what possible relevance does Bowen's research, completed more than five decades ago, have for practice today? The problem of psychosis and its related difficulties (i.e., negative symptoms) remain a concern today. In addition, parents continue to express concerns about their children and to seek professional treatment to help them. In anxious situations, children and adolescents are still hospitalized. Bowen's concept of the family as an emotional unit, and how that relates to symptomatic members, is today a standard perspective in family therapy.

The Family Study Project produced many significant findings that are relevant today. Three of the most significant are the interrelated development of the concept of the family as an emotional unit, the related developments of family psychotherapy, and the emergence of a new therapeutic role. The overall purpose of this work is to bring to light some of Bowen's original papers from the Family Study Project relating to the development of these important contributions.

Bowen, however, was not the first person to note that the family was a social and emotional unit. For example, an early example was Ackerman (1937), who wrote an article early in his career entitled, *The Family as a Social and Emotional Unit*. However, Ackerman's article was more sociological in nature and discussed the general considerations of family unity, foundations of the family, environmental effects, internal organization, and the emotional life development of the family.

Bowen's concept of the family as an emotional unit was based on observational research and is more specific than Ackerman's. The concept offered details on how family members affected one another emotionally and physically. In addition, Bowen evaluated and developed a new method of working clinically with families, termed family psychotherapy, which derived from that concept.

Like others who studied at Menninger's after the Second World War, Bowen initially trained as an analyst. Working in this way, he became very emotionally involved with his patients. He also gained expertise in the management and interpretation of transferences and counter-transferences with a wide variety of patients including schizophrenic patients and their families. However, his thinking about the nature of the therapeutic relationship began to change.

> An important part of all family research and family therapy has been the ability to put the schizophrenia back into the family and keep it there permanently, while I serve as a consultant, or a coach-scientist outside the family emotional system (Kerr & Bowen, 1988, pp. 370).

What are the implications of viewing the family as an emotional unit and focusing the therapy (i.e., family psychotherapy) on the family unit? Family psychotherapy, according to Bowen, was one solution to a "therapeutic dilemma" (Bowen, Dysinger, Brodey, & Basamania, 1957). This referred to the therapist psychologically assuming a parental role with patients. The dilemma was resolved if the therapist worked to avoid a "parental role." But if the therapist worked to avoid this involvement, then who would fulfill this role? Bowen's conclusion, made during the Family Study Project, was that it should be the patient's own family. Also, Bowen and his colleagues in the project attempted to focus on the mature side of the patient while the immature side was lived out in their family. However, they found it was not always that straightforward.

A second implication was the healthy respect Bowen and his colleagues had for daily dealing with very intense family relationships, specifically the family conflicts and their impact upon the staff. Intense emotionality within families did not vanish in 1959; their impact on family members and with psychotherapists continues today. Bowen and his colleagues found that it took "great skill and training" to work hourly and daily with these "complicated intense relationships." Summarizing this challenge for the staff, he noted, "In our experience, the greatest problem is the unwitting response to the immature side in spite of all effort to control this" (Bowen, 1956c, p. 4). This effort was challenging, and the project staff found that it would be easier if they worked to avoid the symbiotic conflicts rather than directly engage them. The effort was to remain supportive yet neutral. Through trial and error, a daily patient-staff group was found to be the best method of keeping these conflicts contained within each family and help with staff over-involvement.

Because of the successes of the patient-staff groups, all individual psychotherapy for the patient and parent(s) were discontinued. It was these early patient-staff groups, later termed family psychotherapy, that attracted the most attention of numerous visitors to the project.

A third implication of Bowen's NIMH Project concerns the nature of the therapeutic relationship. If the therapist can overcome the obstacles presented by a clinical and emotional awareness of the concept of the family as an emotional unit, then the traditional therapeutic relationship is significantly altered. Bowen found that it is possible to work clinically with families from a position of emotional objectivity and detachment. This in some ways is analogous to the traditional position of analyst to patient. Relating to the family unit necessitates avoiding over-involvement with individuals within the family. Bowen's project also clearly demonstrated that you could be helpful to families without enhancing and interpreting transferences. The papers selected for this book tell the story of the history of this transformative development known as family psychotherapy.

OUTLINE OF THE CHAPTERS

The papers selected for this volume are some of the most significant completed during the Family Project that deal with the specific factors that influenced the early development of family psychotherapy. Comments precede each chapter.

Chapter 1 has two papers on the problems in managing symbiosis with the staff and project families. Chapter 2 contains four papers highlighting the emergence of the cornerstone concept of the family as an emotional unit, and chapter 3 highlights a seminal paper from July 1956 on the origins of family psychotherapy and a new therapeutic role with families. This paper contains a detailed discussion of the management of transferences and counter-transferences when working with family units.

Chapter 4 offers important contributions from a capstone workshop presented in 1958 near the end of the Family Study Project. In 1958, Bowen and his colleagues conducted a workshop called *The Psychotherapy of the Family as a Unit*. Unfortunately only the paper by Dr. Bowen survives from this workshop. However, there is a unique and valuable transcribed copy of comments made by participants after all the presentations. Chapter 5 contains a second important workshop in 1959, called *The Family as a Unit of Study and Treatment*. There were four papers presented by Dr. Bowen, Dr. Brodey, Dr. Dysinger, and Betty Basamania, MSS. All the papers were published in 1961 in the *American Journal of Orthopsychiatry* and permission has been graciously given by John Wiley & Sons to reprint them in this book.

Chapter 6 presents a paper termed "The Prospectus." This paper was completed after the project ended for a grant that unfortunately never materialized. It is an exceptional overview of the Family Study Project. Chapter 7 is a discussion of some of the seminal contributions of Bowen's NIMH Family Study Project. Last, chapter 8 is a summary of family psychotherapy as understood during the Family Study Project.

ACKNOWLEDGMENTS

I am indebted to many individuals for assistance with this long-term project. Ruth Riley Sagar, M.A. and Michael Kerr, M.D., both of the Bowen Center for the Study of the Family, were very helpful with my research proposal to the History of Medicine Division of the National Library of Medicine. Drs. Michael Kerr and Daniel Papero of the Bowen Center have provided invaluable contributions for many years on the topic of family psychotherapy and personal coaching. John P. Rees, M.A., MLIS, Curator, Archives and Modern Manuscripts, History of Medicine Division, National Library of Medicine, and his staff were always helpful and thoughtful in answering questions and emails, providing prompt and much-appreciated assistance with the boxes of documents, and promptly sending copies of requested papers.

Catherine Rakow, MSW, the original Bowen archivist, was the first person to work on and organize Dr. Bowen's papers before they were given to the National Library of Medicine. She gave an excellent presentation on her work to my Postgraduate Seminar in Bowen Family Systems Theory and its Applications that captured my interest in this area. Collaborating with her has been greatly rewarding. Clarence Boyd, MSW, was helpful in answering questions about how to access the papers in the History of Medicine Division, and encouraged my efforts to continue work on the project papers.

My research seminar at the Bowen Center for the Study, directed by Kathy Kerr, RN, MA, read various drafts of this and past-related work. Their comments, thoughts, and encouragement were very helpful. I also appreciate the editorial comments by Cathie Parkhurst and Chad Vickers, Ph.D., of Rose Street Mental Health Care. A very special debt is owed to Rachel Butler, my daughter-in-law, who re-typed most of the original documents, and to our youngest son, Jeremy, who gave hours of graphic design suggestions and telephonic computer assistance. Lastly, a great deal is owed to Amy King, an acquisitions editor at Rowman & Littlefield Publishing Group, Inc. for her patience, and long-term support of this project.

The vagaries of private practice at Rose Street Mental Health Care, with no-shows and late cancellations, presented opportunities for writing and thinking during the day. Last, and certainly not least, is my wife "Sam," who with few complaints supported my work on this project during the evening hours and weekends. She also made valuable manuscript comments, especially on grammar. I owe her a great deal in this endeavor and throughout our lives together, traveling the world with the U.S. Air Force and now in north Texas. Lastly, thanks to my grandchildren Courtney Ann, Mary Allison, Joshua Thomas, and Grace Manning King; Natalia Paolina Butler; Molly Marie Ojeda; and our newest family member, Jacob Martin Butler, who joined our family in May, 2011. They are constant reminders of the reality of the concept of the family as an emotional unit.

1

The Problem of Managing Symbiosis

INTRODUCTION

These reports are some of the earliest on Bowen's live-in Family Study Project. The Project Description Sheet is the first report written in December 1954, two months after the project began. The second is an Interim Report on Research Project completed in May 1955.

The Family Study Project began with two mother-daughter dyads residing full-time on a specialized inpatient research unit. The initial goal was to study and observe mother-daughter dyads over time. The dyads were chosen based on "who had intense infantile attachments to mothers who were available to spend all, or a good portion of their time, in the hospital with the patients" (Bowen, 1954, p. 1). Mothers and daughters were chosen because the facilities were better suited for women (Bowen, 1954).

The objectives were clearly outlined. The project was designed to gather data on mother-daughter intense attachments assumed to impact the child's emotional development and schizophrenic symptoms. Another objective was to evaluate whether the participation of the patient's mother was useful in the treatment process. The method utilized was observation of the dyads with minimal staff interference. Traditional psychoanalytic psychotherapy was also provided for each mother and daughter dyad.

The initial project description sheet from December 1954 indicated that the ward setting could be successfully adapted to the mother-daughter dyads.

The Interim Report on Research Project was completed in May 1955, about six-and-a-half months after the project began. The title *Influence of the Early Mother-child Relationship in the Later Development of Schizophrenia* describes the focus at that time. Notable is an early description of

"complicated staff relationships." Bowen concluded, "We anticipated staff
tensions. We did not anticipate them being as formidable as they have become. At times the tensions reach an intensity that seriously threatens the
structure of the project" (Bowen, 1955a, p. 2). Bowen referred to the difficulties that staff had in daily managing the symbiosis with project families.
The intensity within the first three mother-daughter dyads significantly
impacted the staff. In fact, this was a problem that had to be resolved so the
research could move forward.

Program Description Sheet
December 1954

Interim Report on Research Project
May 1955

December 1954

Analysis of NIH Program Activities
Project Description Sheet

1. *Institute*—National Institute of Mental Health
2. *Laboratory or Branch*—Clinical Investigations
3. *Section*—Adult Psychiatric
4. *Location* (if other than Bethesda)—
5. *Serial No.*—143 (C)
6. *Project Title*—Influence of the early mother-child relationship in the
   later development of schizophrenia.
7. *Principal Investigator* (s)—Murray Bowen, M.D.
8. Other Investigators—Ervin Goffman, Ph.D., William C. Jenkins, M.D.,
   Lyman Wynne, M.D., Robert Dysinger, M.D., Mrs. Thais Fisher, Social
   Work.
9. Project Description

Objectives: This project is directed at an area of growing evidence that
certain conditions exist in the very early relationship between mother and
infant which sets the stage for certain lifelong intense attachments between
mother and child which impedes the child's development into adult emotional
maturity, and which may set the stage for the later development of clinical
schizophrenia. The project is designed to gather more detailed data, to help
validate or disprove existing ideas about it, and to check the belief that the
presence of mother is beneficial to the treatment of schizophrenia.

Methods employed: To bring patient and mother together in a structured hospital ward where an attempt is made to maintain the most ideal treatment environment. This permits a maximum of readily available observations in a setting where the emotional climate can be more easily defined and controlled, and where there is minimal interference of external environmental forces on the primary–patient relationship. Both mother and daughter are provided with psychotherapeutic relationships to help define the emotional problems of each.

Patient materials: The group is kept small to provide an intense study over a long period. Two young women were selected who had intense infantile attachments to mothers who were available to spend all, or a good portion of their time, in the hospital with the patients. Women were chosen because the ward settings adapted itself better for women. A third pair will be added in early 1955, and a few others may be added as facilities and staff permits.

NIMH
Serial No. 1/2 (C)

Major finding during the year: After two months, the project would appear to be more promising than anticipated. It has been easier than expected to structure a favorable ward setting. The observational material has been favorable, the initial improvement has been surprisingly good. Whether improvement is inherent in the method remains to be seen, but it appears that the presence of mother is a major factor in the improvement.

Significance to mental health research: There are indications that this may be one of the most important areas of psychiatric and psychological research. Few settings other than the Clinical Center could provide either the facilities, the staff, or the atmosphere for such a project.

Proposed Course of the Project: This entire area of investigation is big and vague and largely unexplored. This project might well be a kind of pilot study to point the way to many more detailed and specific studies in the future. This project itself might be expected to continue several years.

May 1955
Interim Report on Research Project

1. *Institute*—National Institute of Mental Health
2. *Laboratory or Branch*—Clinical Investigations
3. *Section*—Adult Psychiatric
4. *Location* (If Other Than Bethesda)–
5. *Project Number*—
6. *Project Title*—Influence of the early mother–child relationship in the later development of schizophrenia.

7. *Principal Investigator* (s)—Murray Bowen, M.D.
8. *Other Investigators*—Olive Quinn, Ph.D., William C. Jenkins, M.D., Robert Dysinger, M.D., Morris Parloff, Ph.D., Mrs. Thais Fisher, Social Work

Interim Report

I. Goals of Study

The project is directed at the growing evidence that certain conditions exist in the very early mother-infant relationship which impede the child's emotional maturation and set the stage for the later development of clinical schizophrenia. The goal is to secure more precise information on the mother-infant relationship. The method is to bring these chronically immature adult patients and their mothers together in a treatment setting. The hypothesis is that there is an intense interdependent need between these mothers and patients, that the phenomenon has many similarities to the original mother-infant relationship, and that the character of relationship can be altered in a specific treatment milieu which can control some of the factors which originally made the relationship necessary.

II. Description of Data Already Collected

A. Voluminous recorded raw observational data on the character of the relationship between mothers and daughters.

B. Recorded psychotherapy hours with the patients and recorded interviews between social worker and the mothers.

C. A most favorable clinical response in all the patient-mother groups. Any one of these patients would be considered a poor therapeutic prospect in the usual clinical setting. It would seem that we can expect a favorable result in all of them. Whether or not the research formulation is the most logical, the predictability of response would indicate some soundness of approach.

D. A mass of recordings of staff meeting in which we are attempting to work on the very complicated staff relationships among the people connected with the project. We also have the recordings of supervisory meetings where we have attempted to formulate the dynamic process within the staff. We anticipated staff tensions. We did not anticipate them being as formidable as they have become. At times the tensions reach an intensity that seriously threatens the structure of the project. This data is becoming big enough and important enough to become a separate project on its own.

E. Sociological data collected by and used by the sociologists studying group dynamics in a hospital setting.

III. Further work, facilities, and time to complete the study.
    A. Further Work
        1. Much more attention to establishing and maintaining an adequate, consistent, controllable, and predictable ward milieu. The problem of staff tensions has to come to some moderate resolution before the original research plan can go on at reasonable efficiency. The clinical improvement of patients in spite of our own emotional ineptness is gratifying.
        2. Systematic working up of collected data. In some areas the data is too voluminous. In others it is deficient. Working up of data should enable us to focus more precisely on the problem.
    B. Additional facilities and personnel desirable
        1. More time from a sociopsychologist. The size of the problem in establishing a milieu could use half the time of such a person. Dr. Parloff has done a fine job with a small amount of time. A sociologist does not have the clinical interest nor training for this.
        2. A research assistant. A qualified person to collect and classify data. Negotiations are under way for this person.
        3. A clinical assistant to the principal investigator. This should be a younger physician who could do records, take care of patients' physical needs, and do innumerable other such duties.
        4. An interested senior psychoanalytic consultant. Preferably this should be an analyst who can respect schizophrenia and who can be objective about the project without over-praising it or without becoming over-critical of the departure from conventional procedure. A request has been made for Dr. Lewis Hill.
        5. About ¼ time from an interested clinical psychologist. His point of view and orientation is most valuable. His help with testing and other such procedures is of lesser importance.
        6. A full time occupational therapist. This has been discussed with O.T. Eventually we will get this person.
        7. Eventual transfer of our principal clinical center services—social work, nursing, occupational therapy—from clinical center supervision into our own Institute.
        8. The usual and often repeated need for adequate recording facilities.
    C. Additional time
    This study could go on indefinitely. At this point the plan would probably be to go on until we can come out with some reasonable answers, or until we hit a block that is too much for us. The first block on establishing a milieu is formidable. We run into conventional nursing, social work, and other practices that give way slowly. The nursing problem may be the biggest. Our other professional people

we pick carefully. In nursing we take all applicants and still cannot fill our vacancies. This project proposes to make maximum use of the nurse as a mother figure and yet we find ourselves using nurses who have difficulty in this area.

IV. Estimation of Project

The project has been in operation 6½ months. Results to this point have been gratifying. This whole area of investigation would appear to be a rich one. The side areas that present themselves are many. We believe the general hypothetical framework with which we started to be sound. Much of the data collected thus far seems to fit into the general hypothesis. In spite of the difficulties encountered, there is a general air of hopefulness and enthusiasm in most of the people associated with the project.

2

The Emergence of the Concept
of the Family as an Emotional Unit

INTRODUCTION

This chapter includes four unpublished papers from 1955, 1956, and 1957. These include a Project Description Sheet, two Individual Project Reports, and an unpublished paper on the Family Project.

The Project Description Sheet from December 1955 is significant because of the major findings. That is, the comment noting the "growing awareness" of family members that might be important to the mother (Bowen, 1955b, p. 2). Bowen also concluded "the mothers can shift more rapidly when the father can begin to shift and increase helpfulness to her" (1955b, p. 2). In addition, there were continued comments about the challenges of working with the family intensity of this magnitude.

In the section on the proposed course of the project, there was the first mention of including fathers or other important family members in the family research. In fact, the first family group with both parents and their child was admitted during the later part of 1955. A significant change in direction also occurred. As Bowen (1955a, p. 3) described, "a shift from seeing schizophrenia as a process between mother and patient, or as an illness within the patient influenced by the mother, to an orientation of seeing schizophrenia as a distraught family that becomes focused on one individual." Thus, the project changed from studying mother-daughter dyads to one focused on the family unit.

The change in the direction of the Family Study was reflected in the title of the Annual Individual Project Report of 1956 (Bowen, 1956a). The title was *The Study and Treatment of Schizophrenia as a Family Problem*. This report was completed 26 months after the onset of the Family Study Project. The project description on the first two pages presents a concise summary of the project. The report outlines how the focus changed based on the observation of the first three mother-daughter dyads. An interesting observation was as follows:

> The psychopathology fluctuated in a way to suggest "first the schizophrenia is in the patient and now it is in the mother" and the area of the problem shifted in a way to suggest first the problem is between mother and patient and now it is between mother and the rest of the family (Bowen 1956a, p. 2).

The project was redesigned to admit family members important to the mother-daughter relationships. This perspective helped conceptualize schizophrenia as a family process rather than something only in the patient. Small families were selected and hospitalized and the therapeutic effort was directed to the family as a group rather than the individuals within the group.

There were three final important observations in the 1956 report. The first is that all individual psychotherapy was discontinued and the therapy was instead directed to the family unit. Second, it was noted that the families tended to "spray" their anxiety onto the staff resulting in the families becoming calmer but the staff getting upset. Third, there were examples of the patient's symptoms decreasing in response to an increase in emotionality of their sibling.

The next paper was called *The Family Project* (Bowen, 1956b). This is based on the similarity to another important paper completed in the same year. Notable in this paper was an early discussion of the development of daily family groups that today would be called a variation of multiple-family group therapy. These groups included all patients and project staff.

An important principle was responsibility for self rather having staff take over parental functions. "The staff attempts to stay neutral and supportive, without taking sides, and to stay out of the family differences" (Bowen, 1956b, p. 4). It was found that this task was exceptionally difficult for staff, but if staff could do this, there was an increase in maturity of the family members and lessening of the family emotionality absorbed by the staff. "As the group took on increased importance in the therapeutic effort, staff members roles moved away from the traditional roles" (Bowen, 1956b, p. 4). This is a reference to the daily staff-family groups. It is also the first mention of a new role of the family psychotherapist. The family groups also reduced the intensity of transferences and kept the "original family relationships intact" (Bowen, 1956b, p. 6).

An Individual Project Report was completed for the calendar year 1957 some 38 months after the project began. This report noted that after the first two years there were major changes in the hypotheses and treatment. This was the first year of no major changes. However, some decisions were made to respond to clinical demands. One such decision was to place all the family members in multi-family groups. "The group was a means of reducing transference to a minimum and of keeping the original family relationships intact" (Bowen, 1957, p. 6). A major finding of this report was termed "family group reaction patterns," where the families present "a group picture of helplessness and inadequacy" (Bowen, 1957, p. 13).

Project Description Sheet
December 1955

Individual Project Report
1956

The Family Project
1956

Individual Project Report
1957

R.P.C
December 1955

Analysis of NIH Program Activities
Project Description Sheet

1. *Institute*—National Institute of Mental Health
2. *Laboratory or Branch*—Adult Psychiatry
3. *Location (if other than Bethesda)*
4. *Serial No.*—NIMH 170 (C)
5. *Project Title*—Influence of the early mother-child relationship in the development of schizophrenia.
6. *Principal Investigator (s)*—Murray Bowen, M.D.
7. *Other Investigators*—Robert Dysinger, M.D., Mrs. Betty Basamania, M.S.W., Mrs. Charlotte Schwartz, M.S. (Since December 1, 1955)
8. *Project Description*

A detailed clinical study of a small group of severely impaired psychiatric patients and their mothers. Patient-mother pairs are chosen who have intense emotional attachments to each other of the type found in many chronic or severely impaired patients. The patients and mothers are treated in an environment designed to bring about improvement in patients and a decrease in the intensity of mother-patient attachments. The setting permits detailed objective observational data of the multiple facets of these complicated relationships.

Objectives:

   a. To define and substantiate to degree of importance of the mother in the development of schizophrenia. It is hypothesized that emotional needs in the mother not fulfilled in other relationships brings about the intense mother-child relationships and that these individuals, who go on to adulthood with some degree of unresolved attachment to their mothers, are the ones who develop clinical schizophrenia and other such severe psychiatric illnesses.

   b. To further check and develop the treatment program which was developed from the original hypotheses.

Methods:

   a. To bring together in a treatment setting several patients and their mothers in whom the attachment of mother to patient has continued. During the 14 months since the project was started, female patients have been used because we believed the ward would adapt itself better to women.

   b. To put these mother-patient pairs on a ward where psychoanalytic principles determine the development of the treatment environment and psychotherapeutic principles are used in treating the individual patient and mothers. This brings both mother and patient into a setting where the relationship can be influenced by the environment and where direct objective observations are possible.

Patient Material:

Three mother-daughter pairs have provided the main core of clinical material. In addition there has been briefer and less intense work with some six or eight patients with problems in this general area. Mothers either live with their daughters on the ward or live nearby and participate actively in the daytime treatment program.

Major Findings:

   a. More rapid and more solid clinical improvement in the patient when the mother is treated with the patient than when the patient and mother are treated separately or when patient is treated alone.

b. Continuing data that would seem to support the hypothesis that the origins of schizophrenia belong somewhere in the early relationship between the mother and the infant.

c. A different kind of data when mother and patient are put together with the major emphasis on treatment than has been reported when the main object has been observation of the relationship.

d. A rapidly growing awareness of the importance of father or other family figures important to the mother. Patients who did not improve when treated alone, could begin to respond favorably when the mother began to make some response to treatment. It would appear that mothers can shift more rapidly when the father can begin to shift and increase his helpfulness to her.

e. An ever-increasing respect for the difficulties of getting a staff together and welding it into a smooth working unit capable of dealing with a problem of this intensity.

Significance to Mental Health Research:

There have been growing indications for the last ten years that the early relationship of the mother to the infant is of great importance in the development of schizophrenia. As far as is known, no one else has ever approached the problem by actually bringing the mother into the hospitals with the patients. The expense involved, the high degree of clinical flexibility required, the staff requirements, and the necessary hospital facilities make this into a project that would be difficult to impossible in a less well staffed and equipped setting than the Clinical Center. The first year of the project, which has been largely an exploratory period, has been most promising. There are indications that this can be an area that will lead to redefining our old concepts of schizophrenia and to new treatments approaches immeasurably more effective than psychotherapy.

Proposed Course of Project:

a. To include fathers or other close family figures within the groups to be studied or treated. One such family group with the father living with the mother and patient on the ward was admitted in the last days of 1955.

b. A shift from seeing schizophrenia as a process between mother and patient or as an illness with the patient influenced by the mother to an orientation of seeing schizophrenia as the manifestation of a distraught family that becomes focused in one individual. The course will be to see the project as a "family project" rather than a "mother-patient" project.

c. The mother-patient study will be continued but in the context of the family group rather than an isolated entity within itself. In brief, it seems that the mother-patient relationship is the axis in the development of the patient's incapacity, but that other relationships are important in influencing the mother-infant relationship.

d. Breaking down the main project into several sub-projects to more adequately work out details in smaller areas.

e. An increase in research staff to take over the responsibility for sub-projects.

f. Continuation of the main project as a kind of pilot study to help define important areas. It is proposed to keep an adequate balance between the pilot study and the more definitive sub-projects.

g. An attempt to work out techniques to be therapeutically helpful to the family as a unit rather than isolating the various family members for individual help through psychotherapy.

Individual Project Report

Part A. Project Description Sheet

1. *Serial Number* - NIMH-AP-1 (C)
2. *Institute or division*— NIMH-CI
3. *Laboratory, Branch, or Department*— Adult Psychiatry Branch
4. Section or Service—
5. Location (If other than Bethesda)—
6. Project Title— Study and Treatment of Schizophrenia as a Family Problem
7. *Principal Investigator*— Murray Bowen, M.D.
8. *Other Investigators*— Robert Dysinger, M.D., Warren Brodey, M.D., Betty Basamania, M.S.W.
9. If this project resembles, complements, or parallels research done elsewhere in the public health service (without interchange or personnel, facilities or funds), identify such research: (by serials no. (s) if within NIH).

This project does not resemble or parallel any other project. There are a number of other projects, including NIMH Project, M-1-011, that study the various family members of the schizophrenic patient but there are no other projects using the theory and methods of this project.

10. *Project Description*:

The project was started 26 months ago. The title through the first year was "Influence of the early mother-child relationship in the development of schizophrenia." The hypothesis was that there is a specific series of events set in motion by the personality structure of the mother which in turn results in the personality configuration in the patient which predisposes the patient to clinical schizophrenia in later years. The thinking was that the psychopathological entity of schizophrenia in the patient developed in response to a kind of nonclinical psychopathological phenomenon in the mother. The theoretical structure in the beginning further hypothesized that there would be a more favorable therapeutic response in the patient if the mother could also be in an efficient treatment program. The project was not designed to test the hypothesis but rather was set up to get clues and impressions about this broad area. To initiate the project, three schizophrenic young women and their mothers were brought into intimate daily living contact in the hospital setting. Clinical experience during the first 14 months was that the relationship patterns between mother and patient pretty much followed the hypothesis but beyond this, the psychopathological structures of mother and patient were not as discrete and fixed as we had believed and the relationship patterns did not remain between the two as had been hypothesized. Instead, the psychopathology fluctuated in a way to suggest "first the schizophrenia is in the patient and now it is in the patient and now it is in the mother" and the area of the problem shifted in a way to suggest "first the problem is between mother and patient and now it is between mother and the rest of the family." In accord with this the project plan was changed to also admit fathers and other key family members who played important roles in relation to this central mother-patient relationship. To make it as simple as possible, admission was restricted to small families to permit the entire immediate family to live on the ward. There seemed to be an operational advantage in seeing schizophrenia as a process within the entire family rather than a fixed state within the patient. The main focus remains on the mother-patient relationship. The addition of other family members makes it possible to observe their participation in the mother-patient relationship.

a. Objectives: The study and treatment of the entire central family group in families with a severely schizophrenic son or daughter. The goal is to bring the entire central family group into a living situation where relationship patterns can be observed and studied and where therapeutic forces can be directed at the family problems.
b. Methods: Select small families in which there are few members in addition to the central father, mother, schizophrenic patient triad. These are also to be families relatively separated from "in-laws" or other compli-

cating close relationships. This is to permit hospitalization of the entire immediate family group if the occasion necessitates. The families live full time on a psychiatric ward. The disruptive influences in such families and the problems of having a psychotic patient within the family group are of such intensity that it would be hard to furnish enough help to enable the family to stay together outside a hospital setting. The therapeutic effort is directed toward the family as a group rather than individuals in the family group. This comes from the experience of having disruptive forces become more intense when family members isolate and individualize problems. The orientation to the theoretical formulations and toward the therapeutic approach is a psychoanalytic one.

  c. Patient Material: The following table is a schematic configuration of the four families in the study who were admitted when the focus was on the mother-patient relationship. There were two other "mother-patient" families who dropped out during 1955. It will be noted that the first family was on an outpatient status until they left Bethesda for a summer vacation together. Both members have lived on the ward since each returned to the project. The time estimates are approximate in terms of psychological participation. For instance patient Number 1 was listed administratively as an in-patient for 4½ months in 1956 when her participation was more accurately that of outpatient.

Table 2.1.

Family Member	Sex	Age	First Admitted to Project	Outpatient Status	Time in Months on Vacation	Live on Ward
Family No. 1						
Patient	F	33	Nov. 1954	4½	2½	5
Mother	F	59	Nov. 1954	4½	4	3½
(Pt. and mother have occasional contacts with divorced father and married older sister).						
Family No. 2						
Patient	F	18	Nov. 1954	—	—	12
Mother	F	54	Nov. 1954	—	—	12
(Father and mother divorced 15 years— almost no contact with him. No other immediate family)						
Family No. 3						
Patient	F	22	Dec. 1955	—	—	12
Father	M	52	Dec. 1955	—	—	12
Mother	F	44	Dec. 1955	—	—	12
Sister	F	15	Feb. 1956	1	8	3
(Normal)						
(Above is entire immediate family)						

Family Member	Sex	Age	First Admitted to Project	Outpatient Status	Time in Months on Vacation	Live on Ward
Family No. 4						
Patient	M	20	Aug. 1956	—	—	4½
Father	M	44	Aug. 1956	—	—	4½
Mother	F	44	Aug. 1956	—	—	4½
Brother	M	14	Aug. 1956	3		4½
(Normal)						
(Above is entire immediate family).						

d. Major Findings:
1. Marked differences between what family members say and what they do in relation to each other. The verbal report often becomes a defensive exact opposite of what really went on between them.
2. Inability of family members to distinguish feeling from reality. This is not constant in all family members but the phenomenon is much greater in these families than other families.
3. Major family decisions made more to allay the anxiety of the dominant one in the family than on objective reality bases.
4. Repeated instances of the family problem shifting from one family member to another. The most constant pattern seems to be for "normal" family members to say, "We are normal. The trouble with this family is the patient," and for the patient to respond, "I am abnormal. The trouble with my family is me." In this state, the patient has the greatest anxiety and other family members have low anxiety. When reality distortions are pointed out in the therapy, the person making the distortion becomes more anxious and the patient's symptoms less intense. It is a kind of mechanism which selects the patient as the "black sheep" or "scapegoat" or the "holder" of the family problem. Whether this be a mechanism that figures into the origin or schizophrenia in the patient or a result of the patient's impairment is an important question. The mechanism first became clearly evident after individual psychotherapy was stopped and the therapy was directed to the family as a group.
5. Repeated instances in which the family attempts to "put the family anxiety onto the staff or onto the environment." When this occurs, the family problem is less intense and the staff becomes upset.
6. Examples in which the normal sibling develops rather severe emotional upsets with almost immediate decrease in the psychotic symptoms in the patient.

7. Continuing evidence that the core relationship around which other family relationships revolve is the mother-patient relationship but that this core relationship is more dependent on other family relationships that originally believed.

8. The more maturity and objectivity attained by the staff, the more calmness and objectivity the family groups are able to attain.

e. Significance to Mental Health Research:

The opportunity to hospitalize and treat entire family groups together provides an "in vivo" setting to observe family relationships that have previously been observed largely from an "in vitro" setting. A number of interesting concepts are suggested from the data collected here. The area is big and vague and unexplored. This project is no more than a preliminary exploration and it may take a number of years with many different projects and adequate numbers of families to validate some of the suggested concepts. If concepts do eventually prove workable and valid, they may be the basis for significant changes in the way schizophrenia is viewed.

f. Proposed Course of the Project:

1. Continue the project on the present level for the immediate future.

2. Continued efforts to refine the therapeutic instrument. This is of crucial importance. The first problem was one of helping the staff with training and with attaining enough emotional maturity to be able to make it possible for families with these intense problems to continue to live together and to make it possible for staff to work with the families. Two years of hard work has brought a workable measure of success in this area. Now it is found that the families get stuck on a problem and that they are unable to resolve their problem until the staff has discovered and solved a similar emotional immaturity within its own group.

3. More effort into writing papers and doing presentations about the projects. One of the main values in this is that it forces the staff to clarify concepts that would otherwise remain unclear.

Part B. Budget Data

Table 2.2.

Murray Bowen, M.D.	Full Time
Robert H. Dysinger, M.D.	Full Time or less if he continues his other project.
Warren M. Brodey, M.D.	Full Time
Claire Thompson	Full Time Research Assistant
Lewis Hill, M.D.	Consultant, 4 hours per month
Charlotte Schwartz, Ph.D.	Sociologist (approx. ¼ time for 3 months Jan. Through March 1956)
Herbert Kelman Ph.D.	Sociologist (approx. ⅙ time for months Feb. and March 1956)

Part C: *Honors, Awards, and Publications*

16. List publications other than abstracts from this project during calendar year 1956:
    a. "Schizophrenia and the Family," Murray Bowen, M.D., Paper presented at Annual Psychiatric Seminar, V.A. Hospital, Roanoke, Virginia, October 1956. Being published in book to include all papers at the meeting.
    b. "Family Participation in Schizophrenia," Murray Bowen, M.D. and Warren M. Brodey, M.D., approved for presentation at American Psychiatric Association, Chicago, Illinois, May 15, 1957.
    c. The "Action-Dialogue" in *An Intense Relationship: A Study of A Schizophrenic Girl and Her Mother*, Robert Dysinger, M.D., also Chicago, Illinois, May 15, 1957.

17. List honors and awards to personnel relating to this project during calendar year 1956:
    a. February 1, 1956— "The Role of the Family in Schizophrenia," Murray Bowen, M.D., Informal Seminar, Psychiatric Staff, Walter Reed Army Medical Center, Washington, D.C.
    b. March 9 and 10, 1956— Murray Bowen, M.D., Panel Discussant, Regional Research Conference, American Psychiatric Association, Washington, D.C.
    c. June 1956— Murray Bowen, M.D. "Treatment of Schizophrenic Patients and Their Parents," Informal Seminar, Staff of Sheppard and Enoch Pratt Hospital, Towson, Maryland.
    d. October 16, 1956— "Schizophrenia and the Family"— Murray Bowen, M.D., Robert Dysinger, M.D., Warren Brodey, M.D.— Formal Seminar Chestnut Lodge Staff, Chestnut Lodge, Rockville, Maryland.
    e. October 31, 1956— Murray Bowen, M.D., Discussant of paper, "The Effort to Drive the Other Person Crazy" by Harold Searles, Annual Symposium, Chestnut Lodge Research Institute, Rockville, MD.
    f. December 4, 1956— Murray Bowen, M.D.— Informal discussion of the project, Research Staff, Rockland State Hospital, Orangeburg, New York.

The Family Project
1956
The Project was set up at its inception for the study of a limited number of schizophrenic patients together with their mothers. Out of the experience and findings of the original study, the Family Project has evolved. However, from

the beginning, schizophrenia was regarded as a family problem rather than a problem within the individual. The etiological hypothesis for the Mother-Daughter study was the psychosis resulted from the persistence of the primary relationship between the mother and the infant-child into the adult life of the child and that it was perpetuated by the emotional needs of the mother. The way in which the investigators regarded the goals and wishes of the mother and of the child are represented in the following tables.[1]

Table 2.3.

Goals and Wishes	Goals and Wishes
1. To be a good father or mother	To be taken care of, nursed
2. To be a good husband or wife	Freedom from responsibility
3. To be a responsible citizen	Have adequate, all loving, all giving, non-demanding figure always at side
4. To assume responsibility for immature side.	—

Table 2.4.

Greatest Threat	Greatest Threat to Above

Mature be overwhelmed by immature side	1. Loss of all important figure through:
	
	  a. Death
	  b. Might drive figure away
	  c. Figure be pushed away by more powerful sibling or by father
	  d. Others

The study was set up as a treatment project to test out the treatment hypothesis that psychosis is reversible when the mother can relinquish the child. In an attempt to make this possible, the first therapeutic method used was the traditional one of the mother and child each having her own therapist and that the child's therapist was a psychiatrist and the mother was seen in casework treatment by a social worker. Psychotherapy[2] was oriented toward responding to the mature side in the patients,[3] with awareness for the infantile side. In this context, the technique undertaken by the therapist was that "of not responding to the immature and to control the therapist's response by awareness of self and by conscious control. The patient was encouraged to relate as a mature person speaking about his immaturity rather than a person relating with his immaturity. In this way, the mature side, rather than the therapist is the responsible keeper of the immature."[4] (For the technical problems, see source of quotes.) The ward milieu was regarded as an important part of the therapeutic plan. The effort was made to maintain on the Unit as near a "normal" family atmosphere as possible. This was done to facilitate the usual "emotional climate" in which these two persons related to one another and, thus, to add to the accuracy of observations as well as contributing to the therapeutic process. The usual administrative ward[5] rules were minimized because of the way in which mother and child invoked the rules with one another rather than to work upon their problems in relating to one another; i.e. Mrs. P. cannot say "no" to her daughter; the daughter requests to drive her car; mother cannot refuse but does not wish this and she would prefer to borrow a hospital regulation to answer her daughter. In a similar manner, the mother and child used their relationships with staff to escape the problems implicit in their intense relationship.

Daily charting and study of the moves the mother and daughter made, toward one another and toward staff, added to the understanding of the closeness and distance problem between these two people and how quickly one or the other would move to include a staff member when the basic relationship was overweighed with anxiety. Thus, a staff member could, unknowingly, become involved in the mother-daughter conflict. To deal with these situations, the group meetings were inaugurated on the unit [5] and they included all patients and staff connected with the Project.

The group meets daily and members are encouraged to bring any problem, staff or patient, for discussion. The basic philosophy of the Group is one in which each member's vote is equal to that of any other member. This is done in recognition of individual worth and self-esteem. It is an atmosphere in which growth can take place and the ego become strengthened through the use of the individual's capacities. This includes being responsible for self rather than having staff take over the lives of the patients which can happen when we expect others to do as we think they should do. The staff attempts to stay neutral and supportive, without taking sides, and to stay out of the family differences. Actually, this is extremely difficult to do for it amounts to resisting a response to infantile helplessness with mothering and firm direction. As a Group continued, there was a marked increase in mature functioning of patients and less of the family conflict was absorbed by the staff.

As the Group took on increased importance in the therapeutic effort, staff member's roles moved away from the traditional roles. As the work continues, we will want to define the roles of the various professional disciplines represented in the Group. For instance, the doctors have moved out of their authoritative role in so far as their responsibilities will permit this; the nurses and aides have moved from the mothering role, the occupational therapist and the social worker have moved from work with individuals to work within the Group.

There were interim findings, growing out of the experience with the Group and concomitant research observations, which brought about the shift from the Mother-Daughter Project to the Family Project. Through the study of the three mother-daughter relationships and testing these findings against our etiological hypothesis (see pg. 1) we became interested in how, within the framework of family, the mother's emotional needs might be met to enable her to release her child. Thus, it was for therapeutic and research reasons that we decided to include fathers to test, further, our therapeutic set of circumstances. The first family group, father, mother and daughter, were admitted in December, 1955. They made early bids for individual psychotherapy.

By now, we had enough experience with the Group to believe that it was a potent therapeutic tool which we wished to test further. Concomitantly, we were working upon the clarification of the theoretical aspects of transference, in terms of our experience with it. To state it briefly, "the transference phenomenon in psychotic patients is different from the transference phenomenon in neurotic patients. That one of the major differences is the intensity and the primitiveness of the transference in psychotic patients. In the analyst of the neuroses the patient relates "as if" the analyst is a parent but neither patient nor analyst ever lose sight of the difference between reality and the "as if" status. Schizophrenic patients develop intense transferences, (if at all) and the intensity is the character of the symbiotic relationship of infant to mother."[6] The Group was a means of reducing transference to a minimum end of keeping the original family relationships intact. Families are expected to be responsible for their child and they can ask for help from staff if they wish to do so. On the other hand, if staff believes that they are being drawn into the family conflict and being manipulated by it, they are free to refuse to participate.

There was evidence that family members having individual psychotherapy were not using the group as did members who did not have individual therapy and we moved gradually away from having any individual therapy to concentrating on the Group. With the focus on the Group, further clarification of the nature of things going on in the Group was possible. This may be represented by the following illustration:

[illustration unavailable in original paper]

The small arrows indicate relationships between individuals; the large arrows indicate how the problems at one level can spill over to other levels.

Among other things, the work on the above illustration helped to focus upon the importance of intra-staff problems, to recognize them and, in so far as possible, to work them through. It highlighted, also, the need for awareness of self and how members related to one another, as well as to participate. Upon computation, we found that at the average size Group assemblage, there are 383 relationships in operation.

Research has been geared to the thinking and activities described above. There are three research meetings per week. One of these meetings is devoted to charting, essentially, the areas presented in the last illustration. In this, we attempted to keep in focus both fundamental and specific areas of research interest and, at the same time, to move along with the unfolding panoramic view of people acting and interacting in everyday living.

The second meeting is operational; where interest is upon intra-family relationships; intra-staff relationships; and inter-family-staff relationships. The third meeting is theoretical, to use our data findings in testing our hypothesis and formulating theoretical constructs, and for paper writing.

Our findings are as follows:

1. The first pair quickly improved to a rather comfortable equilibrium in their relationship. They then seemed to be content in a static state of comfortable "clinging to each other." The patient's clinical improvement had been rather satisfactory by most standards and the symbiotic relationships had become symptom free. We might say that it was "too free of symptoms." They were the last 2 members of an original family group of four. The other members had independent lives of their own. It seemed easy for these 2 to remain in the clinging symbiosis. Now they are again moving a little faster but we have felt the process could have been more alive. Slowness we felt was due to:
   a. Psychotherapy did not achieve all we wished for it.
   b. Reality of "2 surviving family members" providing a natural "clinging together" situation. (Following these developments it was decided to stop individual therapy. The P.'s had been non-participants in the group up to that point. The daughter has returned from a disturbance on vacation and she has become active and verbal in the Group. The mother and daughter's feat of closeness is coming to the surface and they are anxious but active about facing their problems in their relationship.)
2. These two were our most impaired people and both are still on the ward after 20 months. The therapists managed to keep fairly mature relationship but very early the daughter was involved in an acted out

intense loving attachment to ward staff and the other either clinging to the daughter who clung to the staff or involved in an intense hostile attachment to ward staff. There has been some fairly satisfactory clinical improvement but we really have not been able to make our treatment scheme work. Reality wise, these two people are isolates and more impaired than the first two. These are among the most skillful people at getting numbers of outside figures involved in acting out their immaturities with them. Operationally, we have not been able to keep the family problems from spilling into the staff.

3. This was the most volatile and in a sense that most intense symbiosis. It was the most intense example of "I can't live with you—I can't live without you" that we have seen. The mother would get close to the daughter. They would fight. The mother would then reject the patient and go to other children with a symbiotic like attachment there. The daughter would act out and force the staff into a close range tie up with her immature self. These closeness-fighting-rejecting cycles repeated. When we finally were able to partially block the mother's retreat to other children, the patient escaped into a pregnancy. Psychotherapy never really worked here. Both mother and daughter demanded actual parental giving from their therapists and they could both find ready "givers" in other staff members. We felt both would have responded to a therapy approach like "I am for you and I will help you fight your battle" but then the symbiosis would have been transferred to the therapy. This experience made us cautious about working with further multiple sibling families until we can understand the process in small families.

4. The B. Family, Mr. and Mrs. B. have had severe marital conflict throughout their marriage. Upon admission, Mr. B. was unsure of himself. Mrs. B. hovered over their daughter, pampered her and had difficulty setting limits. Mr. B. was shut out of the mother-daughter stronghold. He strived to reach Mrs. B. at times failing in this, he tried to reach his daughter. Mr. and Mrs. B.'s differences were often displaced to their daughter. Mr. B. has moved toward decisiveness and this culminated in his standing up to an authority figure on the staff. There followed in 2 days a marked shift to Mr. and Mrs. B. being together emotionally; when they planned a trip together, their daughter erupted and Mrs. B. was ready to retreat but with Group support, they retrenched. This was followed by Mrs. B. being more firm regarding herself with her daughter and letting her daughter have responsibility for pulling out of her illness. The daughter responded by acting out hostility, with physical attacks on the staff. Mrs. B. took a trip to their home; upon return, she had slipped back to her original position but has pulled up in 10 days time. Mr. B. has been protective and supportive to Mrs. B. since her return.

Table 2.5.

Implications of the Project for the professional disciplines involved on it:

1. Psychiatry   )
2. Nursing   )
3. Nursing Aides   ) each do own
4. Occupational Therapy   )

Serial No. M-AP (C)— 1

1. Adult Psychiatry Branch
2.
3. Bethesda, Maryland

PHS-NIH
Individual Project Report
Calendar Year 1957
Part A.

Table 2.6.

Project Title:	The Study and Treatment of Schizophrenia as a Family Problem
Principal Investigator:	Murray Bowen, M.D.
Other Investigators:	Robert Dysinger, M.D., Warren M. Brodey, M.D., Betty Basamania, M.S.W.
Cooperation Units:	None
Man Years (calendar year 1957):	
Patient Days (Calendar year 1957):	2,950 days
Total:	4
Professional:	3
Other:	1

Project Description:

The project was started 38 months ago. The first two years there were major changes in the hypothesis and in the treatment approach to schizophrenia. This is the first year there has not been a major change to include in the annual report. To summarize briefly, the first year was devoted to the study of mothers and patients. The second year was devoted to the study of families with fathers, to a redefinition of the hypothesis, and to efforts to develop a psychotherapy of the family as a unit. The third year went to refinement of the psychotherapy and an effort to define some of the concepts and to write about experiences that had been hurriedly passed over in the emotional turmoil of the first two years. When the project was started there was no previous literature or experience to use as a guide. There was an intellectual conviction that this area could be profitable. The only blueprint, for an operation that would make it possible for normal family members to continue to live in the high anxiety and for staff to work with the project, was theoretical anticipation of problems along the way and some ideas about possible solutions. Many decisions that affected the entire course were fortuitous ones to deal with the emotional emergency of the moment. Such was the decision to put the entire family together into a family unit psychotherapy. Originally conceived as an emergency measure to control uncontrolled emotion, it opened up a new area of observations, techniques and concepts.

Project Description (continued)

Objective

The immediate research objectives is to attempt to define in more detail some of the many promising clinical findings that were by-passed in the emotional emergency of the early stages. The theory objective is further development and refinement of family unit psychotherapy. A therapy objective to reach a more predictable and efficient means or therapy is a crucial part of the project.

Method:

Small complete family groups which include at least father, mother and schizophrenic patient are hospitalized. The hospital setting permits around the clock observation of the family group. The daily family-staff group meetings serve as a means of further check and understanding of the emotional processes within the group, of the emotional conflict between staff and families, of the emotional process within the family, and as a means of psychotherapeutic communication to the family. An inpatient operation is much more difficult to operate than an outpatient operation but the added information and observation is considered essential. On the other hand, there is evidence that outpatient psychotherapy can be more productive than in the inpatient operation. Several outpatient studies have been carried out in order to observe variations and refinements in family psychotherapy. It is possible to try such variations as the use of one therapist with one or more families; or two or more therapists with one or more families.

Patient Material:

Four family groups participated in the 1957 operation. The first was a mother and daughter connected with the project since November 1954. They lived together on the ward into May 1957 at which time they were discharged from the project. They now live at the family home in another state. The second was a mother and daughter who lived constantly on the ward from November 1954, until discharged to outpatient status on October 7, 1957. They live in a nearby city. The third was a family of father, mother, patient, and normal sibling admitted in December 1955 and still active in the project. The normal sibling has been away at school most of the year. The family is currently disrupted by the mother's 3-month "business leave" to their home in another state. The fourth is a father, mother, patient, normal sibling family admitted in August 1956. The family group has been present the entire year except for the normal sibling's absence at school for 6 months. This family may terminate project participation January 1, 1958. An outpatient family of father, mother, and psychotic teen-age daughter have been seen as outpatients since early November 1957. The *four inpatient families are the same referred to in the 1956 report.*

Project Description (continued)

It is expected that 2 new impatient families will be admitted by December 1957, that new families will be admitted as vacancies occur in the ward, and that some outpatient families may be started in 1958.

Major Findings:

1. The clinical facts reported in the 1956 annual report, which could be classed as Intrafamily Reaction Patterns are still as prominent and pertinent as a year ago. These are part of many such observations awaiting more careful definition and incorporation into papers. There is a new series of observations to suggest that the psychotic symptom in the patient is an outward expression of a regressed impulse in a parent.
2. A new class of prominent clinical findings might be classed as "Family Group Reaction Patterns." The families present a group picture of helplessness and inadequacy. They deal with many life problems as burdens to be endured rather than problems to be solved. Therapeutic emphasis is directed at this helplessness. When either parent is able to become active in solving such a problem, the emotional adjustment of the entire family changes. The schizophrenic patients have responded favorably to actions by parents that popular concept would call traumatic. This suggests that it is not traumatic action but passive lack of action that is incapacitation to patients.

Significance to Mental Health Research:

It may be that the broader perception of psychological processes provided when the family is seen as a unit, may be a major contribution from this project. A medical orientation to help the patient places the fact of a parent's activities in regard to the patient in a completely different perspective than when the orientation is toward helping the family unit. When the project staff is able to achieve a family unit orientation, the investigator has the experience of observing what appears to be a new psychological phenomenon. If it is possible to clarify some of the profusion of clinical facts observable from this perspective, this might become the basis for a different view of interpersonal processes.

Proposed Course of Project:

1. Complete the evaluation and organization of data already secured.
2. Continue the inpatient operation with 3 to 4 complete small families using the same theoretical orientation and treatment approach as a year ago.
3. Build up an outpatient service for variation and development of therapy techniques and to complement the inpatient service.
4. Make an effort to define and conceptualize some of the major clinical findings by-passed in the effort to establish the project.
5. Seek help from other disciplines in the further effort to conceptualize and validate findings.

Part B included: Yes

PHS-NIH
Individual Project Report
Calendar Year 1957

Part B: Honors, Awards, and Publications
Publications other than abstract from this project: None
Honors and Awards relating to this project:

1. "Study and Treatment of Five Hospitalized Family Groups each with a Psychotic Member." Invitation to present paper about project to Section on Intrafamily Relationships.
2. "Family Participation in Schizophrenia," Murray Bowen, M.D., Invitation to speak to Psychiatric Staff, Phipps Clinic, Johns Hopkins University, Baltimore, March 12, 1957.

3. "A Psychological Formulation of Schizophrenia," Murray Bowen, M.D., Invitation to speak at a panel discussion on the Etiology of Schizophrenia, American Psychiatric Association, Chicago, Illinois, May 15, 1957. This has been elaborated into a chapter of a book, *Studies in Schizophrenia* to be published in the Spring of 1958.
4. "Family Participation in Schizophrenia," Murray Bowen, M.D., Presented at the Meeting of the American Psychiatric Association, Chicago, Illinois, May 15, 1957.
5. "The Action Dialogue" in *An Intense Relationship: A Study of a Schizophrenic Girl and her Mother*, Robert Dysinger, M.D., Presented at the Meeting of the American Psychiatric Association, Chicago, Illinois, May 15, 1957.
6. Invitation to speak at the Zurich Conference— not accepted.
7. "Schizophrenia and the Family," Murray Bowen, M.D., Invitation to present paper about project at Iowa-Nebraska Psychiatric Meeting, University of Iowa, Iowa City, Iowa, October 26, 1957.
8. "A Working Approach to Schizophrenia and the Family," Murray Bowen, M.D., Invitation to present paper on working research concepts at a research seminar, Yale University, New Haven, Connecticut, October 31, 1957.
9. Group for the Advancement of Psychiatry, Family Committee, Murray Bowen, M.D., April 5, 6, 7, 1957. Invitation to meet with Family Committee. November 7, 8, 9, 10, 1957, Murray Bowen, M.D., Invitation to become permanent member GAP Family Committee.

NOTES

1. Bowen, L.M., M.D., "Formulation of the 3 East Project, July 16, 1956."
2. The use of the word "psychotherapy" includes both psychotherapy and casework.
3. The use of the word "patients" refers to both mother and child in this paper.
4. Bowen, L.M., M.D., op. cit., pg. 4.
5. The words "ward" and "unit" are used interchangeably.
6. Bowen, L.M., M.D., op. cit., pgs 1 and 2.

3

The Beginnings of Family Psychotherapy

INTRODUCTION

This chapter includes one report called *Formulation of 3 East Family Study Project July 16, 1956*. This is the longest of any report and is considered a seminal document. In this, Bowen presents a detailed background of the theory and clinical details of the patient-staff groups that eventually became known as family psychotherapy.

His opening argument is that transferences with neurotic and psychotic patients are different. With psychotic patients, the transferences tend to be very intense and primitive. In the traditional therapeutic relationship, it was the function of the therapist to psychologically replace the parent. Noting the difficulty in this area, and in an understatement, Bowen states "that it requires great skill and training for a therapist to work successfully with these complicated intense relationships" (Bowen, 1956b, p. 2).

Bowen's (1956b) overall objective was to work to reduce the intensity of the transference with psychotic patients and keep them on the level of neurotic transferences. In addition, a secondary goal was to avoid the therapeutic role of psychologically "replacing the parent." However, there was an important caveat. That is, his approach works best with patients who have some degree of contact with their families so the problems can be lived out within their family.

Bowen (1956b) also illustrated a model depicting the schizophrenic patient as having both a mature and immature side, that is, "two contrasting dichotomies." Several illustrations are presented to represent the dichotomies.

"In general, the immature wishes are synonymous with infantile striving for dependent security, and the mature wishes are the mature wishes of any of us" (Bowen, 1956b). In the therapeutic interaction:

> The patient is encouraged to relate as a mature person speaking about his immaturity rather than a person relating with his immaturity. The therapist is free to relate at length to the mature side about the problem the mature side has with the immature side. In this way, the mature side, rather than the therapist, is the responsible keeper of the immature. (Bowen, 1956b, 4)

Several important results were identified from the mother-daughter project that began in 1954. One was that the symbiosis in the mother-daughter dyads remained there "uninfluenced" until this relationship changed. Second, the therapist's goal was not to become involved in the symbiosis of the family. Last, it was recommended that the staff would assume a neutral and supportive role. Individual psychoanalytic psychotherapy for each family member was discontinued. However, the psychological symbiosis remained a problem and "tended to get stuck to ward staff" (Bowen, 1956b, p. 5).

Noting the benefits of the daily patient-staff groups, Bowen stated:

> A combination patient-staff group was started as an operational procedure. It was designed as a technique to keep tensions contained within each family group or at least to prevent the symbiotic like attachments from attaching themselves to the staff. (7)

The first staff-patient groups were started in December 1955. The results were significant.

> It was the first time we have been able to keep these primitive intra-family attachments reasonably contained with the family group. At time of high staff tensions, the family problems spill temporarily into the staff but this has been clinically manageable for the first time. (Bowen, 1956b, p. 8)

The overall treatment philosophy became one of staying "out of immature attachments . . . to be helpful while staying detached from the other person's immaturities" (Bowen, 1956b, p. 9). The staff-patient groups had both an operational and a therapeutic side. It was operational because it helped in the early identification and remedy for staff over-involvement. It was also a therapeutic endeavor. The groups followed a predictable course. That is, initially the focus of the parents was primarily on the patient and their problems. Over time, parental differences surfaced, and when these were resolved, changes followed in the patient.

Formulation of 3 East Family Study Project
July 16, 1956

Formulation of 3 East Family Study Project July 16, 1956
Objective:
The treatment of schizophrenia using modifications of psychoanalytic techniques and extension of psychoanalytic theory.

I. Methods:
    General statement: The postulations and formulations around which the project is organized are about as follows:
    1. That the transference phenomenon in the psychotic patient is quite different from the transference phenomenon in the neurotic patient.
    2. That one of the major differences is the intensity and primitiveness of the transference in the psychotic patient. One author expressed it by saying "As the oedipal conflict is nuclear to the neurosis, so the symbiotic conflict is nuclear to the psychoses." To put it another way, the transference in neurotic patients has qualities in common with the relationship of the oedipal child to the parent while transference in psychotic patients has qualities in common with the relationship of the infant child to mother.
    3. That the development of and the analysis of the transference is one of the major treatment methods in the analysis of the neuroses. To summarize it in terms of the analytic process, it might be said that the analyst psychologically replaces the inadequate "bad" real parent as an adequate understanding "good" parent figure. The relationship to the analysis has qualities that make it a replica of the patient's early parental relationships (transference). Through the working out of this unreal relationship to the analyst the patient gains both an understanding of self and of the early parental relationship. The structure of the classical analytic situation with the frequency of appointments, the passive nonparticipation of the analyst, and the free association of the patient very quickly brings about an ego regression and the establishment of neurotic transference. The patient's ego structure however is sufficient that the transference remains on an "as if" basis. The patient relates "as if" the analyst is a parent but neither patient nor analyst ever lose sight of the difference between reality and the "as if" status.
    4. That the development of transference in the psychotic patient has many significant differences. So great are the differences that the early analysts believed the schizophrenic patient to be incapable of

transference. We know that this is incorrect. The schizophrenic patient is incapable of transferences in the same way as neurotic patients, but schizophrenic patients develop very intense transferences and the intensity is of the character of the symbiotic relationship of infant to mother. The neurotic patient relates with a feeling of helplessness and "as if" he were helpless. The psychotic patient "knows" he is helpless and relates with helplessness in the relationship. Whereas the analyst's passive understanding of the neurotic conflict is sufficient for the development of neurotic transference, the psychotic patient will demand "show me you are interested" and he may withhold a relationship until he is shown. The analyst in adapting techniques to meet this situation, can actually engage in doing things a parent would do, to the point that is possible for the analyst to be acting out the parent's role and the patient to be acting out the child's role. The psychotic patient is not as capable as the neurotic patient in maintaining the treatment relationship on an "as if" basis.

5. While the various methods and approaches to the psychotherapy of schizophrenia have not generally been structured in this general scheme, it might be said that the most successful approaches do employ variations of this principle which is one of the important principles in the analysis of the neuroses. It might be said that it is a goal that the therapist replace the parent in psychological importance and that a major therapeutic principle is the analysis of this relationship. Sechehaye has had successes in which she has actually replaced the parental figure to the point of taking patients into her own home as a member of her family. Tosen has done this also while he has used other techniques that are quite different. Much of Federn's work has also been in this area while he has written about and stressed other points. Fromm-Reichmann has emphasized the importance of the refinement of the therapeutic instrument (analyst) to eliminate counter-transference problems while she has also developed techniques to very precise level in an effort to bring more success to this difficult relationship. This project would make no attempt to evaluate or compare therapeutic principles. It would merely say that it requires great skill and training for a therapist to work successfully with these complicated intense relationships, that the intensity and character of transference is one of the difficulties, and that it might be worthwhile to focus some study on it.

II. Specific Methods
   General statement:
   1. The specific approach to this project would go in the direction of attempting to treat schizophrenia by techniques which attempt to keep the transferences on the level of intensity of neurotic transference. A general theme comes into focus. One point would be that the therapist might develop techniques in which he did not lend himself to the patient's bid that he do a certain amount of "replacing of the parent." Experience would indicate that the patients do in fact need such a figure. If this be so, then who should this figure be? To what extent is it not so?
   2. There are indications that technical variations directed at this point work better for the better integrated patients who in fact are in living contact with parent, spouse, sibling, child or other such figure with whom they already have an intense interdependent relationship and that such variations are least effective with hospitalized patients and those out of living contact with such figures Some formulations obtained in experience with the better integrated type of patient has some bearing on the overall problem.
   3. That the schizophrenic patient is often a strange combination of the impaired infant and the adequate adult. The mature and infantile goals and wishes can exist side by side in stark contrast or in strange mixture. At this point we assume a model about as follows. The patient is shown in two contrasting dichotomies.

Table 3.1.

Goals and Wishes	Goals and Wishes
1. To be a good father or mother	To be taken care of, nursed
2. To be a good husband or wife	Freedom from responsibility
3. To be a responsible citizen	Have adequate, all loving, all giving, non-demanding figure always at side
4. To assume responsibility for immature side.	—

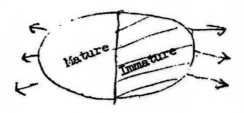

Table 3.2.

Greatest Threat	Greatest Threat to Above
Mature be overwhelmed by immature side	1. Loss of all important figure through:
	a. Death
	b. Might drive figure away
	c. Figure be pushed away by more powerful sibling or by father
	d. Others

In general the immature wishes are synonymous with infantile strivings for dependent security and the mature wishes are the mature wishes of any of us. The same model of course can apply to the neurotic patient except the dichotomy is much more subtle and less openly manifested and the intensity of the immature side has much less urgency.

4. That a model of psychotherapy with a schizophrenic patient, and using this kind of a treatment scheme might be as follows.

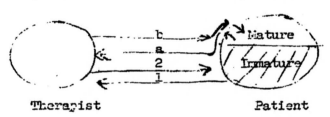

In general the patient is usually in the role of the impaired one in relating to the therapeutic figure and he usually will present his immature side to the therapist. This is represented by arrow (1). It is not too difficult for the therapist to respond to the patient in kind—as if the patient was in fact infantile. This is represented by the arrow (2). The technical scheme here is not to respond to (1) and to control the therapist's response (2) by awareness of self and by conscious control. The patient is encouraged to relate as in arrow (a) as a mature person speaking about his immaturity rather than a person relating with his immaturity. The therapist attempts to relate always to the adult in the patient arrow (b) and he is free to relate at length to the mature side about the problem the mature side has with the immature side. In this way, the mature side, rather than the therapist is the responsible keeper of the immature. There are of course hundreds of technical details concerning this but this is the overall scheme. One of the serious technical problems is when the patient appears to be ALL immaturity and it is essentially impossible not to respond to the immature side for a time. In our experience, the greatest problem is unwitting response to the immature side in spite of all effort to control this.

5. That this scheme seems to work best when there is a close figure in living contact with the patient with whom the patient keeps an already existing symbiotic like relationship. To say it another way, it is easier for the therapist to keep the therapy relationship directed at more mature levels when there is an already existing intrafamily relationship with whom the immature level can be "lived out." The scheme appears least successful when the patient's life is essentially devoid of such figures. It is then difficult for the therapist to be anything except an actual "one and only" figure to the patient. It would appear also less successful when outside figures are cut off by hospitalization or other such separation and there are a number of hospital staff personnel identified with the therapist who "act out" an over protective relationship in response to the patient's immaturity.

II.   Specific methods

Specific statements:

1. That the "mother-daughter" project started in November 1954 has as one of its goals that the symbiotic relationship between mother and daughter remain there uninfluenced until something changed within the relationship itself, that the therapists would find it easier not to become incorporated into the symbioses, and that the ward staff stay neutral and supporting and above all to stay out of the symbiotic conflict. The following is the general model of the plan.

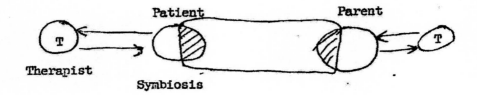

The individual psychotherapy was to be the primary therapeutic method. The milieu was designed to support without taking sides. Theoretically we felt this would be therapeutically successful if the immature symbiotic sides of both patient and mother could stay contained within the two of them. It did not work this well. Operationally, the "symbiotic sides" of both patients and daughters tended to get stuck to ward staff. This kind of helplessness is a very sticky thing as we see it, and it is easy for it to attach itself to protective mothering or firm direction.

2. The following was our experience with the original three mother-daughter pairs:

   a.

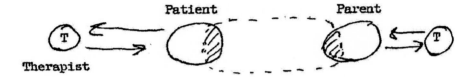

This first pair quickly improved to a rather comfortable equilibrium in their relationship. They then seemed to be content in a static state of comfortable "clinging to each other." The patient's clinical improvement had been rather satisfactory by most standards and the symbiotic relationship had become symptom free. We might say that it was "too free of symptoms." They were the last 2 members of an original family group of four. The other members had independent lives of their own. It seemed easy for these 2 to remain in the clinging symbiosis. Now they are again moving a little faster but we have felt the process could have been more alive. Slowness we felt was due to:

1. Psychotherapy did not achieve all we wished for it.
2. Reality of "2 surviving family members" providing a natural "clinging together" situation.

   b.

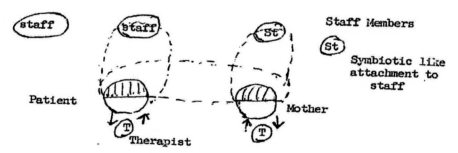

These two were our most impaired people and both are still on the ward after 20 months. The therapists managed to keep fairly mature relationships but very early the daughter was involved in an acted out intense loving attachment to ward staff and the mother either clinging to the daughter who clung to the staff or involved in an intense hostile attachment to ward staff. There has been some fairly satisfactory clinical improvement but we really have not been able to make our treatment scheme work. Reality wise, these two people are isolates and more impaired than the first two. These are among the most skillful people at getting numbers of outside figures involved in acting out their immaturities with them. Operationally, we have not been able to keep the family problems from spilling into the staff.

c.

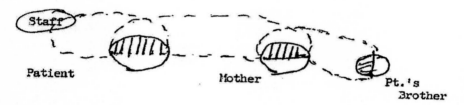

This was the most volatile and in a sense the most intense symbiosis. It was the most intense example of "I can't live with you—I can't live without you" that we have seen. The mother would get close to the daughter. They would fight. The mother would then reflect the patient and go to the other children with a symbiotic like attachment there. The daughter would act out and force the staff into a class range tie up with her immature self. These closeness–fighting–rejecting cycles repeated. When we finally were able to partially block the mother's retreat to other children, the patient escaped into a pregnancy. Psychotherapy never really worked here. Both mother and daughter demanded actual parental giving from their therapists and they could both find ready "givers" in other staff members. We felt both would have responded to a therapy approach like "I am for you and I will help you fight your battle" but then the symbiosis would have been transferred to the therapy. This experience made us cautious about working with further multiple sibling families until we can understand the process in small families.

3. A combination patient-staff group was started as an operational procedure. It was designed as a technique to keep tensions contained within each family group or at least to prevent the symbiotic like attachments from attaching themselves to the staff. The group included all the patients and all the staff. The group

met daily. The meeting was structured more as a family council than the usual group meetings and members were encouraged to bring any problem, staff or patient, for discussion. Other meetings, where such things could be discussed, were discontinued to "force" problems into the group to bring about as open and mature functioning as possible. This meeting we consider to have been one of the more successful operational changes. There was a marked increase in the functioning maturity of patients as well as staff. The leakage of intrafamily problems into the staff group was decreased and more definable but it still persisted.

No one really knows what constitutes this thing we call symbiosis. No one has ever described it satisfactorily except a Tennessee Williams or a Fans Kafka: To be able to live with it is an achievement. To understand it scientifically is a goal.

4. Husbands and fathers were missing. Here were 3 mother-daughter pairs from marriages from which husbands had been long divorced. The first mother had no one except the patient and there she clung. The second could do no more than cling to daughter who clung to staff or to try to cling to staff herself. The third shifted her clinging from patient to other children to welfare workers. We decided to also bring in fathers along with mothers and patients. If the mothers and fathers could resolve problems until they could "have each other," perhaps some of our operating difficulties could be solved.

5. The first mother-father-patient group was admitted in late December 1955. (The patient-staff group was running fairly well.) The patient had not even acknowledged introduction to the project director before she made a strong bid for him to "take me out to lunch." Within 2 days, all three family members were making these bids for individual relationships among ward staff. To prevent what we perceived as a rapid dispersion of family tension to the staff, we asked the father and mother to forego their bids for individual psychotherapy and to utilize group meetings for discussion of their problems. This scheme has worked faster and smoother than any plan to date. It is the first time we have been able to keep these primitive intrafamily attachments reasonably contained within the family group. At time of high staff tensions, the family problems spill temporarily into the staff but this has been clinically manageable.

III. Plans for the future
1. Admissions
   a. General. Admit additional mother-father-patient family units to the physical capacity of the ward (3 or 4 families). (It has been surprising and gratifying to find fathers so willing to take leaves of absence from work and so eager to participate.)
   b. In general the following criteria are proposed for selection of families.
2. Patients either men or women and severe chronic schizophrenics. Would prefer fairly young and vigorous patients who have a lot of energy to put into a fight against illness. A chronic fairly fixed illness would imply, according to our hypothesis, that the relationship problem in parents is pronounced.
3. Parents as young, healthy and vigorous as possible. Would prefer those as involved with patient as possible and preferably those who have need to interfere in previous treatment attempts. Would prefer parents in forties or early fifties who still have fight and need to achieve an adjustment for themselves. Vigorous parents in their fifties probably to be preferred over complacent parents in their forties.
4. Families generally to have one or two siblings. We are interested more in the size of the intense inner family constellation rather than a fixed figure. A large family might have reduced itself to a small inner group and thus be small in a psychological sense. A small family might have intense in-law attachments and thus be psychologically large.
5. Be able to admit the other sibling or other close family members for visits and brief stays. A visit from such a person can therapeutically "shake-up" slow moving relationships between the mother-father-patient group.
6. Treatment Plan
   a. The primary focus is on the family problem rather than individual problems. (It is hard to tell anyone, who has the problem. Family members tend to accept none of the "blame" or too much of it.) We expect the family to maintain itself as a unit and for the father and mother to be responsible for attentions, disciplines, and personal care of the patient. In other words, the family maintains its normal intra-family relationship con figuration and we attempt to have the ward structure interfere with this no more than necessary. The staff stands ready to help them, to "baby sit" for their son or daughter if they request and

the daily group approves, and to help them solve their problems but the staff does not assume directions of their lives or to take over anxiety arousing responsibility.

b. Therapy philosophy. The primary philosophy revolves around the thesis in the first part of this write up. In one way it is a negative approach—"Stay out of immature attachments." This is more precisely said "To be helpful while staying detached from the other person's immaturities." It is in helping with a problem without becoming responsible for the problem. Most people in this kind of environment want to be helpful and they try hard to be. Our technical problem therefore is very small in being helpful and very great in preventing over helpfulness. Our basic philosophy would say that our greatest help is in helping people to define their dilemmas. Our greatest energy goes into preventing staff from trying to solve dilemmas. The main therapeutic agent is the patient-staff meeting.

c. Patient-Staff Meeting. This is a daily one-hour meeting of all patient and staff members. It has provided our most effective technique thus far for dealing with these intense family problems without having the family problems leak into the staff group. The model is as follows—

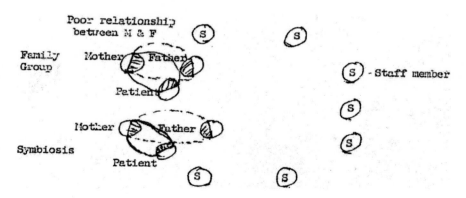

The group is now both an operational and therapeutic group. It is operational in that it is the most effective means found thus far for dealing with daily family problems without someone getting and staying over identified, over protective, or over involved with a single family member. The group does not prevent the involvements. It offers a way of seeing them early. We have developed clinical signs which we can now recognize as indicators of an involvement between a family member and a staff member. The goal is to define and detect the involvement early, else "acting-out" follows, the pattern of family relationships get lost in overwhelming feelings and family progress stops. Staff tensions result in almost immediate staff involvements with patients. Detection and the handling of these are difficult and it requires daily vigilance, experience and objectivity to discover and deal with them early.

The group is also a therapeutic group. Thus far there has been no problem in patients bringing all problems to the group. Each parental difference has roots that go back into the personality functioning of both father and mother and it is easy for the two to start on a simple difference of opinion about the patient and end up in a free going discussion of his or her personal life. The long-term value of this group is still an unknown quantity. How far it can go is still to be determined. At present it is producing results superior to what could be expected in individual psychotherapy. Right now we think of it in terms of "analyzing" the personality functioning of mother in relationship to father and father to mother rather than in terms of single relationship to a therapist. We have question about the size of the group. Thus far we have operated satisfactorily in a group of about twenty people. How far we can enlarge this is still to be seen. This is different than the usual group therapy session in that the primary intense family group is in the big group as a unit and not as individuals. Individual psychotherapy has now been discontinued for all members. There seemed to be something contrary to our basic concept of seeing the family as a unit when individual members' energies and thoughts were directed to self rather than the unit. As to whether individual neurotic problems can go on to resolution in the group or whether these will do best with later individual psychotherapy is still to be left to future experience. We have seriously considered individual family psychotherapy in terms of a family unit meeting with two therapists (one cannot stay free of entanglements) but it is too early to include this in the project plan. Our plan for this project is to add new family members to present group.

d. Projected therapeutic course. In the beginning parents focus on the problem within the patient. Gradually parental differences completely dominate the picture reaching a higher and higher level of difference. Comes a point when one makes a "decision" and moves to a higher level of functioning to be followed by anxiety and eventually change in the other. When parents reach a new stage, then the patient changes. If our thesis be correct, the patient grows out of schizophrenia pretty much alone after the parental shift.

IV. Research Plan

1. The research goal is the treatment of schizophrenia involving:
   a. Hospitalization of mother-father and patient
   b. Techniques that (1) keep the intense primitive relationships within the family rather than "transferring" them to another person, and (2) treat family as a unit.

2. Data Collection
   a. Beginning treatment
      1. Individual family members by psychological tests and individual psychiatric examination.
      2. Estimation of family's mode of functioning as a unit.
      3. Attempt to relate to a and b and b to a
   b. Continuing process evaluation
      1. Daily evaluation of individual adjustment.
      2. Daily evaluation of family group function.
      3. Attempt to relate a to b and b to a
   c. End of treatment
      1. Individual evaluation by psychological tests and detailed psychiatric examination.
      2. Evaluation of family group functioning
      3. Attempt to relate a to b and b to a.

3. Means of data collection.
   a. A and c remain pretty much as details of doing individual evaluations and then evaluations of group function which involves chiefly their manner of relating to each other.
   b. The second section on the on-going process is the important area for which a chart has been devised on which we have the following material recorded daily.
      1. Brief summary of patient's individual functioning
      2. This done for each member of group
      3. Daily note of family relationships.
      4. Summary of total patient-group functioning
      5. Brief summary of patient-staff meeting.
      6. Brief summary of staff functioning, which includes staff relationships that might affect patient group functions.
      7. Notes of relationships of project staff to environment.

In this way we have daily brief records of the on-going dynamic process on each individual, the relationship of individual to family, of the patient group to staff, and of staff to extra ward environment. The data on patients and families provides materials for the family study, and the data on staff and outside groups provides information on the total operation. These charts are summarized at monthly and quarterly intervals in an attempt to extract the most meaningful data.

c. Patient staff meeting. This is our most important sources of theoretical and operating material. On this we have:
   1. Full tape recordings
   2. Two daily meeting summaries done by
      a. Non participant observer
      b. One done by Dr. Bowen to record his impression of the ongoing process.

Especial attention is given to important relationship shifts. Just as in individual psychotherapy one begins to develop a capacity to recognize important landmarks, so it is in working with a group such as this. For instance an individual's relationships remain essentially the same for long periods and then comes a sudden shift. For instance, a patient who has responded in a certain way to the mother will suddenly speak angrily to the nurse for the first time. This focuses special interest on what may be a beginning major shift in her relationship to her mother. The relationships shifts go directly to the family figure involved in a "contained" family and to staff members in a "non contained family."

What we hope to accomplish:

1. Evaluation before treatment.
2. Definition in a controlled way of the techniques in treatment
3. Evaluation or results
4. Material for a number of descriptive reports on various aspects of relationships with these families.

4

The Capstone Workshops

The 1958 Psychotherapy of the Family as a Unit Workshop and Discussions

INTRODUCTION

This chapter presents papers from workshops held near the end or after the close of the Family Study Project. These presentations by all the principal investigators offer a detailed review of the project and for that reason are termed capstone workshops.

The first workshop includes three presentations given on March 7, 1958, in New York, at the American Orthopsychiatric Association Meeting. The first was by Betty Basamania, MSS, the second was by Warren Brodey, M.D., and the final presentation was by Dr. Bowen.

However, as with many archival collections, they are not perfect; sometimes papers are missing. Bowen's paper is the only one located from this workshop. But with disappointments, come surprises. In this instance there are two. The first is the content of Bowen's paper; it is an unusual case study of 85 hours of outpatient family psychotherapy. The second is quite remarkable. The discussions of all the papers were recorded and transcribed. The discussions follow his paper from the workshop.

Bowen's paper on the *Psychotherapy of the Family as a Unit* in 1958 begins with a discussion of the "family as a unit" concept:

> The actual change to this form of therapy was motivated by clinical necessity. It required the difficult clinical problem, created by the presence of parents and patients living together on the ward, to motivate the effort toward family therapy (Bowen, 1958, p. 1).

The central goal of family psychotherapy was clearly identified. It was the analysis of the intense family relationships "in situ" rather than the "transfer" to the patient-therapist alliance. In fact, Bowen cautioned that techniques to enhance a traditional therapeutic relationship should be avoided. Bowen assumed that is was possible to work towards "an objective analytic relationship" to the family unit. Bowen (1958) then presented an 85-hour case study of a family that he felt was successful in family psychotherapy. As far as is known, this report is his only case study.

The transcript of the discussion recorded reactions after all of the presentations by Ms. Basamania, MSS, and Drs. Brodey and Bowen. Interestingly, Virginia Satir was one of the participants. The questions and answers provided additional rich historical material. There was also a general summary of the discussions following the audience comments.

Psychotherapy of the Family as a Unit
Murray Bowen, M.D.

This is the last of 3 presentations to workshop #31, American Orthopsychiatric Association Meeting, New York City, March 7, 1958. The first presentation was by Mrs. Betty Basamania and the second by Dr. Warren Brodey (neither included in this compilation).

The concept of "the family as a unit" was presented to and discussed by this workshop this morning. The background material, distributed to each of you, describes some of the theoretical thinking behind the concept "the family as a unit," and also the circumstances that led to the development of a technique for family therapy. To state it very briefly, the theoretical thinking had been going in this direction for some months. On the basis of clinical material, it seemed to make good sense to look at the family in this way. The actual change to this form of therapy was motivated by clinical necessity. It required the different clinical problem, created by the presence of parents and patients living together on the ward, to motivate the effort toward family therapy.

The professional group has made an effort to define "family therapy." It is clearly differentiated from individual psychotherapy and also from group psychotherapy. The effort is to relate to the family as a single organism. This has required great effort because we are all trained in the problems of the individual, the entire body of psychoanalytic knowledge is oriented to the individual, and it is a most difficult task to reorient oneself.

Individual therapy involves an understanding of the individual in terms of a theoretical concept developed for the individual. An important force in individual analysis is the analysis of the transference relationship between the patient and the analyst. The patient becomes emotionally dependent on the analyst. The analyst interprets the situation. The neurotic patient "gets insight" and does something about this unwanted situation. There is a complication to this way of going in the treatment of the psychotic patient. The psychotic patient also becomes dependent on the therapist—the therapist interprets—the dependence continues—the therapist interprets—the dependence continues—the whole cycle can continue indefinitely. A goal of family therapy is the analysis of already existing intense interdependent relationships within the family and to analyze them "in situ" rather than to permit "transfer" to the relationship with the therapist. A necessary technique is that the therapist avoid those things that encourage the individual relationship, and its resulting transference neurosis. This will be discussed in the case presentation. We believe it is possible for the analyst to get into an objective analytic relationship to psychosis in the family and that this is only hopefully possible in individual therapy with the psychotic individual. The other members of the family are there to "look after" the helpless patient. Of course the analyst hopefully keeps an objective analytic relationship to the situation when he is alone with the psychotic patient, but he always has to contend with the potential situation when the patient can become irresponsible and literally force him out of this analytic position and into dealing with, instead of analyzing, a crisis situation. Volumes can be written on "what to do (to keep and help maintain objectivity) when the patient creates a scene." In an analytic relationship to the family, one has merely to sit and analyze the reaction of the family organism when one side of the organism acts up. Family therapy is also clearly differentiated from group therapy.

A group is an assembly of people brought together for therapeutic goals. The group members have no pre-existing relationships. The closest pre-existing relationship may be the one between group member and the therapist. The goal is to understand the individual as he functions in a group of other individuals.

The general principles of this family therapy will be conveyed in the context of the report of a single family group in outpatient family therapy with a single therapist. This is the most simple model of what we have been trying to do. It omits the many complications of three or four family units in a large group of perhaps 20 people. In the large group there are relationship complications from one family to another, between family members and nurses, between family members and therapists, and most important of all—between nurses and therapists, and between therapist and therapist. The functioning of the individual family member is more obscured in the larger group. The particular family to be described is the one in which the functioning of the individual has been in sharpest focus and the most clearly defined. The patient has been able to talk, which adds a dimension not present with the silent patient. It is also the family, among these 10 families, that has made the best progress.

The family to be presented includes a father of 61 years, a mother of 55, and a psychotic daughter 29 years old. The father is a soft spoken fellow who has spent his business life as the owner and operator of a retail store. His greatest worries have focused on finances. He opened his store early in the morning, closed it late, and often worked on the books on Sunday. At home he was a handyman with a shop in the basement and dozens of articles set aside to be fixed when he had time. The mother is a domineering aggressive person who concerns herself with the lives of everyone around her and who has something to say about everyone. She externalizes her life and it "gets on everyone she touches." Her life motto is (the opposite of the father) "make up your mind and do it. If I let myself dwell on my troubles, I couldn't stand it." She is like most of the mothers. We have referred to them as "externalizing their lives." The father is like most of the fathers. He internalizes his problems and those of people around him. He feels responsible for everything that goes wrong but he does nothing about it. His life motto is "Why advertise your troubles. Don't worry. Everything will work out in the end."

There are two children. The oldest is the patient, now 29 years old. The second is a son, now 25, who had a serious neurotic problem in college, who found his own psychiatrist, who did well in treatment, and who is now an engineer on the West Coast. Most of the time, the family has consisted of these four members. One of the father's single brothers lived with them for a time when the children were small. One of the father's single sisters has lived with them at various times in more recent years.

The father met the mother after he was already hard to work as a business man. She lived in another city 150 miles away. He took a "long weekend" to get married. In the early years of the marriage they bought a good home in a good neighborhood. They continue to live there. The pregnancy with the daughter was very early in the marriage. This pregnancy with the daughter was very much like those of two other project mothers with the schizophrenic patient. The mother wanted a baby "for my fulfillment as a woman." The father thought they were not ready for children. She became pregnant and was in immediate conflict between her wishes for a baby and his wishes "not to have a baby yet." When the marriage relationship was discordant, she was tense, anxious, and preoccupied with fantasies that the child would be abnormal. She wished that she was not pregnant and even wished that she might abort. When things were calm between the parents, she was glad she was pregnant and she felt good. Both before and after the birth of this child, her worries went to the child. She did not have the intensity of concern with the second pregnancy.

She has always been the worrisome anxious mother with the daughter. She was a mother who was frequently at school to check up. She worried about the daughter's relationship, that the daughter might be sexually traumatized by some experience at school, that she would be adversely influenced by the wrong friends, that she might not have a good figure, that her breasts would be too large or too small, and on and on. The mother began work as a secretary after the children were adolescents.

In school, the daughter was recognized as a girl with problems but she was an honor student who was aggressively overactive and also very shy and immature. She was also an honor student for three years in college. Her first psychotic break came at 21 years while in college. She returned home and went into analytic psychotherapy five times a week. She became more and more psychotic and was still insisting there was nothing wrong with her. There was much acting out which included running away from home, psychotic telephone calling around town, and other such activity. The family hired a nurse to stay with her. At times one of the parents would stay home with her. There were suicide attempts including one attempt that was near successful. She took sedatives with both parents at home. They broke down the door and found her comatose.

It was about the time of the patient's first psychotic break that the father went bankrupt the first time. He remained out of work the next four or five years and the mother had the only income. They mortgaged the home to finance private sanitarium care. During the next several years they spent the entire amount of the mortgage. In the hospital, the patient was a fighting, assaultive, overactive, patient who spent time in seclusion rooms and packs after hair pulling, clothes ripping, fights with other patients. One time during a discharge from the hospital, she talked the family into permitting her to try for the stage in New York. After more acting out difficulties she was back in the sanitarium.

The family money was now expended and she was transferred to a public hospital. She forced the family into a court hearing to commit her. An old boyfriend from college days had yielded to the parents' plea to drive her to the hospital the first time. She had refused to go with them. He participated in some kind of a false promise to her. She immediately had a paranoid delusion of having been raped by him and him getting the baby and giving it to the girl he later married. He was a practicing young lawyer at the time of the commitment. She attempted to prove the reality of the rape-pregnancy and illegal marriage of the young lawyer in the commitment hearing. After six months in the public hospital, she settled down on large doses of thorazine and went home. She refused to return for outpatient checkups. She remained out of the hospital about six months, able at times to maintain enough social façade to go to town. Under stress there were wild fights with the parents, much gossiping on the telephone with friends about the paranoid delusions. She hired a lawyer to prosecute the former boyfriend. The father had now been back in a new business for about two years. He started this new business by borrowing on insurance and loans from friends.

The therapy started in January 1957. The mother had inquired about individual psychotherapy for the daughter. There was an initial interview with the mother. The agreement was that I would do family therapy with all three family members if they wished it. If not, I would refer them to someone else for individual therapy. The mother, as have been most parents, was enthusiastic about the idea. The working plan was that we would work together as a group. They could quit anytime they wished to. If the patient required hospital care, it would be necessary for them to use public hospital facilities. The mother discussed the plan with the other two. The patient said she did not need therapy—she needed freedom. The father was non-committal. There was another family fight. The mother packed her bag and moved out saying she would return only after they had made the first appointment for family therapy. About 10 days later the father called and softly asked for a family appointment.

Now to the summary of eighty-four hours of psychotherapy covering the next fifteen months. The first basic rule is that the family work on its problems in the hours while the therapist attempts to analyze what goes on between the family members. Therapy was opened by the mother with a recount of the daughter's psychotic behavior. The daughter responded with loud screaming psychotic expressions of denial. The mother would say, "See it's things like this that try my soul." The daughter would respond with "It is things like this that make me scream." The mother's comments kept going in the direction of proving that the daughter was very sick. Each time she used the word "sick" the daughter's anxiety would mount so high that she would shift into the paranoid delusion saying that she would "kill the boy friend" who raped her. When the daughter shifted into the paranoid delusions (it came when her anger at the mother went beyond a certain level) the mother would yell back, "Shut up—they can hear you all over this end of town." Then the daughter would cry, mother would cry, and say it was helpeless and she felt like giving up. Tears, in such a distraught family, can affect the others as much as the one who cries. In response to the mother's tears, the father would attempt to suppress the daughter and say to the mother, "Don't cry. It is not so bad."

This kind of activity went on about 20 hours at 2 to 3 hours a week. There were two hours in a row that went about as follows: The mother would open with a long verbal account which would say essentially that she had been a good mother but the daughter had been a terrible and ungrateful daughter. The daughter would go into a long account which amounted essentially to denying the accusation—then material to prove she had been a good daughter—and then incidents to prove her mother had been a poor mother. The mother would deny the accusation, offer evidence to prove she had been a good mother, and accuse the daughter of being a terrible daughter. The daughter would deny the accusation, offer proof she was a good daughter, and proof that the mother was a no good mother. This cycle repeated, perhaps 10 times in an hour, with some most dramatic historical material. In our experience, if the therapist gets off into evaluation of the material, he can get lost. No two family members will have evaluated the facts of an emotional incident in the same way. The therapist stuck to pointing out the deny-prove-accuse-prove pattern.

The striking thing was the spectator position of the father. In all other families it was the father who would step in, essentially spank both the mother and patient, and take over. Except, when the father did take over, then he would have acquired the responsibility for policing the family which is fair sized bit of responsibility. In another family, the father took over at this point, subdued the son physically, and policed the family. Within three days the son's psychotic expressions had disappeared and the formerly aggressive mother was saying "It is so nice to have a husband who is a man." About a month after the father said, "I can't take it anymore." He gave up the policing, the mother reverted to her picking on the son and the son reverted to psychosis. This had been the pattern in every family and the therapist got into the position of encouraging the father to enter into the family activity. He said he was impressed that the father did not express his opinions on family issues. It could not be that he did not have opinions. The father said softly, "Well I do. I think mother does pick on her sometimes." The mother responded with some vigor to the father, "What was that? What was it you said?" The father said softly, "Well I think you do start some of these fights." The mother said, "Name one. Just name one. Come on. Get specific. Give me just one example." The father turned to the therapist and said, "See I was squelched." The therapist said, "I just sat here and watched you get yourself squelched."

The next hour father was even more helpless. He had never been in a place that he did not worry about finances. The next hour the daughter said, "I am worried about Daddy. He says that the business is in trouble." The father said, "Don't talk about that here. This is for us (the parents) to talk about. Anything you know, you get on the telephone and advertise it to the town." The reality was that when the daughter got angry with her mother, she would call friends on the telephone and tell intimate family secrets like, "You know, Mother and Daddy have not slept together in 17 years. I don't think they have any sex life at all." To which the mother would say that it was none of the daughter's business what her parents did. To which the daughter would say that the fact that the parents did not get along with each other was just definitely the whole crux of the problem. It was also true that the mother has a kind of a reputation for making many telephone calls a day and for spreading secrets from one to another.

In regard to finances, the father said essentially that the business was going bankrupt but that was his problem and let him worry. He was moving actively into the helpless position in the family and pleading for sympathy. The daughter rushed in to support him. The schizophrenic patient is like a sponge for soaking up anxiety from others. There are the repeated examples of mother getting anxious, of her contacting the patient, and the mother's anxiety decreasing and the patient's psychosis increasing. In this case, the patient soaked up the father's anxiety and became more anxious, and more psychotic over the next several weeks. She began to make telephone calls around town to borrow ten thousand dollars to save her father's business. The father began to make arrangements for bankruptcy. Anxiety hit a high level in the family. The patient was the most anxious. She was panicky and very delusional. She made many telephone calls about town talking about the telephone being tapped and the concern that she and her parents were about to be harmed.

During the anxious period the therapist attempted to define the overlap of family anxiety. The father had dropped back to a less responsible position. This made the entire family very anxious. The daughter rushed headlong into a psychotic bolstering of the father. The therapist made comments like, "The daughter is trying to help save the business, but why did she go rushing in with help when the father had not asked for help?" "Her actions say that the father is not able to know when he wants to help." Both mother and daughter said he would in fact let the family down. The father said that both of them were quick to take over his responsibility.

The therapist gave the family permission to hospitalize the daughter if they could not carry on at home. There were comments like, "Many very upset people are not in mental hospital." "People go to mental hospitals when families or society ask for it." "It is not a function of mine to decide when a family member should be hospitalized. It is the responsibility of the family to decide when they can no longer deal with things at home." "Mental hospitals do force a person into some trying experiences but the human organism is capable of growth in having to adjust to difficult situation." After the 26th hour and 10 weeks of family therapy, the mother made arrangements to hospitalize the daughter in a public hospital. There is another basic rule that was not mentioned. This is that the therapist will report all telephone calls and individual contacts with family members at the next meeting of the family unit. This is to deal with the tendency of family members to establish individual relationships with the therapist. This rule had been neglected in the first hour with the family. Within two days there had been individual calls from the mother and the daughter. There had been more such calls the week of the intense anxiety.

The family was required to make its own working agreement with the hospital. The parents had attempted to get the therapist to side with their viewpoint and the daughter wanted support for hers. The therapist interpreted their efforts to have him take sides. The daughter was on a ward for very upset patients for over a month. She fought, screamed, played tricks on the staff, got into pajama ripping fights and spent considerable time without clothes in seclusion. She was especially antagonistic to doctors who called her "sick." This issue of "sick" and "normal" was an intense issue in the family. They later asked the therapist to state his viewpoint. He said it mattered little to him if the daughter was labeled "schizophrenic" then he would label the family "schizophrenic." If the parents are labeled "normal," then he would insist that all members be labeled "normal." The issue dropped there.

Family appointments had been increased three times a week during the anxiety period. After the daughter was hospitalized, the mother reduced appointments to once a week. Another basic rule has been that therapy can continue as long as any two family members came together. The family anxiety was almost absent in the first hour after the daughter's hospitalization. It was as if she had taken the family anxiety with her to the hospital. The daughter remained out of therapy for 10 weeks. Therapy with the parents was remarkably intellectual and uneventful. The father proceeded with the bankruptcy. They talked of bankruptcy, visits with the daughter, and the pros and cons of what the doctors said. The visits with the daughter were a different matter. She was psychotically angry at the mother for "forcing" her into the hospital and "controlling the doctors" who kept her there. The mother's visits with the daughter resulted in explosive scenes. She decided against visiting but saw to it that the father went twice a week. After the visits with the father had settled down, the mother went again. The daughter had agreed to leave off the rape-pregnancy delusion. They went for a drive. The daughter took up another issue about which the mother was equally sensitive. The mother had lost all her hair in a febrile illness when the daughter was a child. The mother had worn false hair for many years. On this visit, the daughter grabbed the mother's hair and threw it into the street in heavy traffic. The daughter made several attempts to call the therapist but she could never get to a telephone when the therapist was free to talk. She sent him one letter to say she missed the hours and she would like him to help her get out. He read the letter at the next family hour and told them that since this was family therapy he would communicate to them to tell her he had received the letter and that she was probably more familiar than he with hospital rules and what would be necessary for her to be discharged. She received Compazine. The anxiety subsided.

The daughter began to request to return to the therapy hours. She and the parents got together with the doctors for her to get an overnight pass from the hospital on the day of the hour. She returned to the group on the 37th hour after missing 10 weeks. After one week she was able to get passes for two hours a week. She was in one of those states of amazing schizophrenic insight but her emotions were very controlled and her insight more on the intellectual side. She then stayed home on a trial visit status. The hospital had offered help in trying to find a job but she wanted to do it herself. Within two weeks after she returned to the group, there was a rapid series of events. The therapist went on a two-week vacation. One week after his return the mother went on a previously planned three-week vacation to see the son on the West Coast. A characteristic of family therapy is that an absence of the therapist makes much less difference than in individual therapy. There were three hours the week before the mother left. During this week the daughter was in a helpless, though not really anxious state in which she conveyed to the mother "I cannot get along without you." The mother felt like cancelling her trip. The therapist asked if it was usual for the mother to treat the daughter like a helpless child. The day after the mother left, the daughter found a job as a receptionist and began to understudy a girl who was resigning. She had little confidence in herself but she and the father got along well together. She handled some difficult reality situations like the day her predecessor in the office advised her to quit before she was fired. She was fired the day before the mother returned. If the mother had been in town during this period she undoubtedly would have been on the telephone to fight the daughter's battles for her. Therapy, during the absence of the mother, was calm and uneventful. The father's unexcited "do nothing" attitude seemed helpful to the daughter in the job. The therapist made comments like, "What will happen if she is fired?—Will she fall apart? Dissolve? Can getting fired be a growth experience?" Therapy continued uneventfully after the mother's return. The daughter said, "My nerve, my imagination, my fight, is all gone. Unless I can get back my fight, I am sunk. It is the Compazine. The world could run over me and I couldn't fight back. It is terrible not to know when you are anxious. It is awful not to be anxious in situations where you should be anxious." She tried to get the doctors to stop the drug. The mother insisted that the doctor continue it.

The daughter, entirely on her own, got a new job within a week after she was fired. The mother had made some changes. Instead of giving advice or becoming over helpful, she began to respond to the daughter's indecision about jobs with, "For God's sake, make up your own mind what you want and do it." Other than minor changes, the family ran into a "bog-down" after the mother's return. The parents neither agreed or disagreed. They just sat. Each would wait for another to start the hours. Someone might say, "Until some-one thinks of a problem, what time does the Ed Murrow show come on?" The family attitude was "We will tell you and you will give us the answer." Several attempts were made to break up the impasse. The daughter was the only one showing much activity. She at least was working, though she would indicate she was doing poorly. At least she introduced the most issues and she was more alive than the parents. The therapist decided to try a period of an in-dividual relationship with her. So, when she put in an individual problem, he responded as one might in individual therapy. She came to life. She liked it. It was an hour of individual therapy with the parents as pleased spectators. The father said "sh-h-h, let's see how he does it." During the week the daughter called twice with helpless individual problems. Once was "Something inside me tells me to resign the office job and get a job as a waitress or dishwasher. Unless I do, I feel the real me may get blocked. Can you help me figure out this one?" The therapist immediately gave up the idea of individual therapy.

The next hour the therapist said he felt the family passively waiting on him, or fate, or time, for answers to their problems. He may have led them to believe he had answers. Actually, psychiatry has never found an answer to schizophrenia, though the premise of family therapy is that the family can find its own answer if they work on it. He said he was going to fall back to take notes and to attempt to analyze what went on between them rather than participating. At the end of the hour the mother said, "Does this mean you will not see us again when you say we have to do this by ourselves?" The therapist asked the others for their perception of his comments. The mother was amazed that she was the only one who heard the comments this way. They began to check individual perceptions with each other after each hour.

The following hour the therapist passed on an observation from the more distant observer's position. He said they had presented three sad stories that made it sound like the family was on the edge of collapse. The daughter, able to work for the first time in years, sounded like she might fold up any day. The mother was worrying about who would support the family if she got sick. Her last medical check showed her to be healthy and she enjoyed work-ing in spite of her words to the contrary. The father sounded like the prophet of doom with his financial worries. In reality two of the three of them were working, they were living comfortably, and any one of the three was capable of self support. The father said he had to pay back his borrowed insurance. He was asked "Why?" He said, "To support my family if I should die." The mother said, "But you don't support your family we support you." The family helplessness decreased slightly.

One other element came into this. This had to do with a changed attitude toward the families both in the hospital and out. There had been dramatic changes in families when fathers assumed more active and assertive positions. This had been the first change in several families. The therapists began to interpret the passivity of the fathers. If this was the first change in the families, then perhaps the process would go faster by focusing on the fathers' passive withdrawal. This came sharply into the picture with another family. The father was acting a little more like a man with strength. She asked him where he got his ideas. He said, "The doctor told me." After this, the therapists decided to stick to analyzing what went on rather than trying to influence passive fathers.

Gradually we began to work toward a technique we still hold. In each family there is an active one who gets things done. In the therapy, the active one works at the problem and the others play a defensive game. Then the other becomes active. The lead keeps shifting from one to another until, as we would postulate it in mature parents, they can shift the lead easily as the situation demands. For the present, we have come to feel that, if there is just one thing for the therapist to do, it is to support the family member who motivates the situation. There are some good examples from the project. These families are indecisive and incapable of many ordinary daily decisions. They have gone through the years begging and getting and following the advice of others. Their efforts with the patient, whether it be firmness, permissiveness, understanding, total push, laissez faire, or other approach, have been equally unsuccessful and yet they keep seeking advice. New families will infer advice if they cannot get it more directly. They have even tried to do things according to the research hypothesis. When the parents are finally able to do things according to their own judgment, they can do things that look traumatic and schizophrenogenic but the patients respond favorably.

So, in reference to supporting the direction of the one who motivates the situation, we would now say to support him in whatever direction he chooses no matter how illogical it might seem. In this particular family, the family lead had been dropped. No one was doing anything. We wondered who was the moving force in the family. It was the mother who set up therapy, it was she who had maneuvered the family into getting to therapy, and she was the breadwinner. So, why not support the mother.

Immediately, the mother began to move out. She moved to an attack on the father. She spoke of how tired she was supporting the father—How did she get there? She had been supporting an unemployed executive, a man who remains an unemployed executive while his family starves. He is too scared of what others think to ask anyone to help. He can't take a job that is beneath him. He is a broke big shot. He has to be president of the company. He is interested more in his own status than helping his family. She listed many ways he had been so sensitive about what others thought that he could not consider the family. For instance, when the kids were small and one would get hurt and cry, he was interested more in what the neighbors would think about the crying than in how much the child was injured.

This was the first real fire between the parents since the patient's psychotic episode. Up to now it had been between mother and patient. The father reacted by saying, "This is how it goes." "When I need your help you starting lashing out. You and your bitter tongue." She responded, "When you need my help! I've been supporting you for years. That's all I've done all my life is help you. Take it easy on you: You want me to support you the rest of our lives!" The father generally in this reacted like Willie Loman, the father in "The Death of a Salesman."

This phase kept up two or three weeks and the father, in response to the mother, passively made some changes. A few weeks later on a trip out of town to borrow some money from family connections, he had a sudden attack of urinary surgery. The father had a prostatectomy a few weeks later. He was in the hospital two weeks and missed three appointments.

The mother was now in the active lead position, the father was in an acceptably invalided weak position and the patient was somewhat neutral, making good progress in her work. The mother, on the first hour the father was absent, went into about four weeks of her greatest progress (about nine months and sixty hours from the start). She became preoccupied with the nature of her relationship with the daughter. She was spending hours thinking about the relationship. She would be sitting at her desk at work and find herself thinking about the daughter. She began to wonder "Now why would I think about her now?" This was different than ever before. Formerly, when she'd think about the patient's hair, she'd either call the patient to talk about it, or begin thinking about a beauty appointment for her. Now, she wondered "Why do my thoughts go to her now?" She concluded that her life was mixed up with the daughter's in some very complex way. When the daughter felt something she felt it too. When the daughter was anxious, she was too—She remembered an incident in the daughter's childhood when the daughter fell and hurt her head. As soon as the daughter began to cry, the mother's head began to hurt in the exact spot the daughter's head was injured. She pondered the way of this. She wondered how to control this. She had been trying to "put an invisible wall between us so she can have her life and I can have mine." She was able now to catch herself in these feelings "at least part of the time." The daughter said that all her life she had been unable to know how she herself felt. She had depended on the mother to know for her. Occasionally she would feel something different from what the mother said she felt. She would discount her her own feelings as inaccurate and feel the way her mother said she felt. This applies to other things. She depended on mother to know how she looked, if her clothes were becoming, if the colors matched, and many other things. Away at college she could have some of her own feelings but if a teacher said she looked tired, she would begin to feel tired. Later, when her psychotherapist suggested she was lonely or angry, she would have those very feelings. When she would return to mother she would promptly lose her own ability to know her own feelings. Then the daughter recounted her own ability to know how the mother felt and thought. The mother arrived at the concept that parents have to be able to let their children lead their own lives. Although she must have heard this hundreds of times, she reacted as if this was a brand new fresh concept that she had discovered for herself.

The mother and patient made much progress on disengaging their selves in this period of the father's absence. The mother was very pleased. The daughter was somewhat anxious. After the father rejoined the group, the mother continued her efforts to lead her own life and to refuse the daughter's bids to have mother make the daughter's decisions. The daughter began making many bids to have mother decide. Mother firmly said, "It's your life. You decide." In the meanwhile the daughter had been quite successful in her second job in which she won the admiration of the fellow employees for her ability to get along with a dominating woman boss. She resigned after three months to take another job in the journalism field—the area of her college training—at a big increase in pay. Her old employer offered to meet the pay scale of the other job if she would stay. They gave her a "going away party," at which she cried, when she left for the new job.

The mother stopped her effort to change herself, the family went into about two weeks of neutral, and then the daughter began moving forward. She suddenly became very popular socially. It was as if the mother withdrew some of her "self" from the daughter and the daughter had this much to invest outside the family. Except, her relationships with men were intense and over-involved ones. She began to go out four to five nights a week and to come home later and later—2:30, 3:30, 4:30 a.m. She began to go to men's apartments. The question of sexuality came up. The mother said, "You are now 29, you are old enough to make up your mind what you want. If you want sex, well go get it and don't bother me about it. All I say is be discreet about it." The father did not openly oppose but deep down he was much opposed. He objected to the hours, to the propriety of going to men's apartments, waking up neighbors at 4 a.m., and trying to work then when she got only three hours of sleep a night.

After about six weeks of this, the daughter called to ask if she could see the therapist alone for 10 minutes at the end of the next hour. The answer was, "No, this is family therapy." "But this is too personal, I have to talk to someone and I cannot do it with my family." The answer was, "There are other psychiatrists in town if you have to talk personally." Early in the next hour she talked about the problem. It was, "The boyfriend wanted a sexual affair. They were neither ready to think of marriage. He thought they would both enjoy it." The mother said, "I don't know anyone but you who is able to decide how often you want to have intercourse. How does anyone in the family have a real problem?" The father chewed his cigarette. The next hour there was more of the same subject. At the end of that hour the therapist did a few minutes directly with the daughter. He asked her how easy or how hard would it be for her to have a sexual relationship. He conveyed that in her, her emotional involvement and sexuality were intimately fused, therefore he did not see how she could toss sex around any more than she could toss friendship around. She had indicated that her goal was marriage. He didn't see how it was psychologically possible for her. He would be interested in knowing how she did it, if she was able to.

The next hour there had been a big family fight. The daughter called the boyfriend to see him. (She had not told the parents it was to terminate the relationship. She did tell them she would return by 1:30 a.m.) The parents returned from a party at 1 a.m. The mother went to bed. At 2:30 the father went to her room to say "She isn't in yet." The mother said, "You woke me up for that!" At 3:30 the father went to the mother's room and said, "It is 3:30 and she isn't in." The mother said, "If you wake me up again you are going to have me to contend with. Go pace the floor, wring your hands, chew cigarettes, walk around the block, do anything you want to only do it quietly but don't wake me up again tonight." At 5:29 a.m., as the daughter and boyfriend walked in the door, the father, who was now cooking eggs for himself, yelled from the kitchen loud enough to awaken the mother on the 3rd floor. "It is now 5:29 and they are just coming in the door. They are coming in at 5:29." In the next therapy hour the daughter calmly said that the thing that got her was the father's lack of guts to come out and speak directly to the boy. He had to stay in the kitchen and scream like a mad child. Of course, she wasn't pleased that he had to get so mad but, if he did get mad, he could at least act like a man about it.

The next hour, the 77th in 53 weeks, was another neutral hour. The daughter in a new hair-do was as beautiful, calm, assured, and as self contained as a young lady could be. The parents were beaming with parental pride and satisfaction. The talk of dates and sex had disappeared. She had terminated the last relationship and had met some of the old gang from college days. At the time of her first psychotic break she had terminated relationships with the old bunch. She felt she would never be acceptable to them again. She had spent

8 years avoiding them. She had ducked into stores to avoid meeting them on the street. She could not risk the pain of their pity and rejection. During the week she had met one of them. Several of the boys were lawyers. She went with them to a reunion at the country club. They knew about her prolonged psychosis but accepted her as if nothing had ever happened. At the club she met a former mental hospital patient who aggressively asked if she had not been in a hospital. Her date who knew about her mental hospital history said, "Sure, she was born in one." She said his consideration in this meant a great deal. New friends asked many questions like, "Where have you been?" "How have you been able to stay single?" She said people are made anxious by former mental hospital patients. She used to be self-conscious and think they were reacting to her but they are really made anxious by their own fears concerning mental patients.

She found herself gauging replies according to the person. To her friends she told the truth, to the nosey ones she said she had been out of town, to the fresh ones she said she had just finished 8 years finishing school at SP and SE. There had been two proposals of marriage in two weeks, one after three dates. She was wondering what would make a boy do something as impulsively as that.

The following 5 hours, the mother, previously the old reliable family Gibraltar, began to shift to the weak, whining, complaining position. She began to pick childish fights with the daughter. The daughter took over half the cooking for the family and chased the mother out of the kitchen on her nights to cook. There was one hour when the mother hurled repeated projections at the daughter who carefully hurled each other back. The mother would cry. The daughter would say, "Well stop trying to dump your troubles on me." The father would attempt to side with the mother and the daughter would split the alliance and deal with each separately. The mother said the daughter could just pack her things and move out. The daughter said, "Someday I will marry and leave but I will leave when I choose and not before." She said, "My emotions would have me sympathize with mother but I have my own life to lead I will not permit myself to react to her emotions." In the 82nd hour the father was beginning to show his first assertiveness and the mother showing a little indication of being able to lean on him.

The mother had become quite the petulant, screaming child. The daughter said she had kept track of the mother's childish temper tantrums and they occurred only on the daughter's night to cook. The mother denied that they were temper tantrums, that she was childish, or that it had anything to do with the daughter cooking for the family. The mother said the daughter screamed too. The daughter said, "Only after 30 minutes. I could restrain myself and not scream at all but I don't want to have to exercise that much restraint. So I give you 30 minutes and then yell back at you." The mother said, "I am not going to pay for any more therapy. F(the daughter) has done well. She is almost ready to go out on her own. She can manage her own life somehow. This (82nd) is the last hour I will pay for." The daughter said she had felt for sometime that she should pay part of the therapy bill. She would pay it from now on only she could not afford but 2 hours a month. The 83rd hour the mother was still the childish one. She attacked the daughter and the father. The daughter said, "Mother, I know you. If I give an inch to your tears, I am sunk. Your sad story leaves me unmoved." The father began to speak up to the mother for the first time. On the 84th hour, the mother opened with a proposition. The daughter had done so well and she was really beyond the ability of the parents to help her anymore. She was suggesting that the parents drop out and the daughter continue alone in therapy. The daughter said, "Mother, what's your angle?" The mother said, with tears and with a fairly sizeable emotional response, "I had only you in mind and I get stepped on like this." The daughter said she had things she wanted to work on for herself but she would rather do it in family therapy. The parents had not changed very much in their relationship. She had spent a lot of years in a kind of crazy mission to help them. She realizes that this was all part of the craziness and she is no longer a missionary to help them, but she would prefer to go on together. The father said he thought this was supposed to be family therapy. The mother said essentially that the parents were too old and fixed in their ways to change. The question worked around to an opinion from the therapist. I said I had not yet worked to an opinion from the therapist. I said I had not yet worked a family through to termination and I had often wondered if eventually it would be necessary for the family unit to break up and do it in individual terminations. They had been able to accomplish quite a bit for themselves in 84 hours. I thought the potential advantages of a group effort far from exhausted. I thought the question, for me, would be a little more to the point if—say the family had a fight—the daughter wouldn't see them—the daughter had been thinking about getting an apartment. I said I had considered the question if it came to this point and my answer would be, "Change to another therapist." The mother was very anxious and tearful the rest of the hour. Both father and daughter were firm and unaffected by her anxiety. The father was getting almost gleeful in his new assertions of strength—with gestures. The mother said, "If you point your finger at me just one more time, I'll bite it." He pointed his finger right at her. She laughed and moved her chair closer to his. The daughter spent the rest of the hour reviewing conversations about impotence and frigidity she had had with boyfriends. At the end of the hour, the daughter asked for my bill. The 85th hour will be April 9, 1958.

Notes on the Discussion in Workshop November 30
Orthopsychiatric Association Meeting
March 7, 1958
Typed by: Alice R. Cornelison

Morning Session—Discussion following the paper by Betty Basamania

Louise Moran: How did the siblings feel about coming into the hospital and to the project and what was their participation?

Basamania: One sibling usually participated. The extent of participation was up to them and up to the family.

Auster: How were the families selected?

Murray Bowen: They were selected originally. Originally the most intense mother-daughter relationships were selected. Then, when whole families were to be studied it was a question of the father who could and would come in.

Winona Chatterton: Did the father work?

Murray Bowen: One found a manager for his store; a second obtained a leave of absence; a third manages a 40 hour work week with a 70 mile round trip drive in order to live in the hospital; the fourth is employed.

Chatterton: What is the effect of the father's working or not working?

Dr. Bowen: The more passive father is not working.

Phyllis Rolfe: What is the physical plant like?

Betty Basamania: The family project has a ward at the National Institute. Superior physical set-up. Recreation program, etc. (She went on to elaborate on this.)

Rolfe: Is there a sense of family unity? (I guess, in the living arrangement).

Betty Basamania: Families divide up the amount of living space among them. They divide up the rooms, eat in the common dining room. There is a kitchen at their disposal. They can make provisions for the impaired member (This was the expression chosen to designate the schizophrenic.) if they choose to be away from the hospital for any time.

2.

Mandel (?) Mad: Are staff roles structured or not?

Basamania: That question will be answered in one of the later papers.

Dr. Zucker: Are these voluntary patients? Is there a charge for their care? What is the community reaction? Are the families classed as patients?

Basamania: Some of this will be discussed later. There is no charge. There has been no community reaction.

Dr. Bowen: In order to eat meals within the hospital one must be designated a patient, therefore a class of "normal controls" was developed, but this could not be used; therefore, there must be a diagnosis and the category for experiment only, has been used.

Dr. Zucker: Did they accept this?

Dr. Bowen: They are all too ready to accept this diagnosis and then live up to it.

Dr. Zucker: Do they buy groceries?

Dr. Bowen: Yes they are allowed to buy groceries and to police their purchase and try to keep the other families out of them, if they can.

Satir: What is the diagnosis given?

Dr. Bowen: Diagnosis is not really wanted and it's not clear. (I think, it's the staff who don't want the diagnosis.)—Then someone answered 0Y0-004 as the classification diagnosis.

Chatterton: Then you do avoid a psychiatric diagnosis?

Brodey: Yes, except for the impaired member, where there would be a legal problem if there were no psychiatric diagnosis. (Then an interchange which I did not get.)

Auster: Is there interaction between family and family?

Basamania: A great deal. Dr. Bowen will discuss it.

Dr. Bowen: These families isolate themselves. They are isolated groups with little communication from family to family. Almost no first names are used, except on the patient level.

Auster: Do they have insights into other family's relationships without seeing their own?

Dr. Bowen: All the time. Very aggressively.

Koepp: Is there a pre-admission work up?

Basamania: They are given the opportunity. They are seen in order that they may be given the opportunity to decide on admission.

Rolfe: How do they react to it? Are they hard to reach?

3.

Basamania: Not all accepted. Families where the patient has not yet been hospitalized have been less willing. These families in the study are some in which they have had experience with many other hospitalizations.

Zucker: Are these multi-generation?

Dr. Fleck: Referred to a Texas study.

Dr. Bowen: There is nothing to contradict that possibility. Referred to Louis Hill's statement, "it takes 3 generations to make a schizophrenic."

Dr. Fleck: Commented here, and I didn't get it down.

Satir: If there is a significant grandmother, for example, is she included?

Basamania: Not to date.

Dr. Bowen: Have looked for families in which the parents and the patient had separated themselves. Mother and father and patient—primary group, an essential threesome.

Dr. Fleck: Do you mean where the grandmother lives in? We have some in which the nuclear family never really formed. The father is running to his mother—the mother to her sister etc; and the center of gravity remains outside the nuclear family.

Rosenblatt: Raised question about staff problems, staff dynamics. Do these people really set as they are diagnosed?

Dr. Bowen: Referred to David Rioch—work on the front lines. Something about it was hard to tell the physically injured from the psychologically impaired, until moved further back.

Brodey: Expectation is part of attitude toward people. These are people in whom the expectation is very important—in whom what is expected of them is very important.

Dr. Bowen: The parents have to do more-calling. The patient soaks it up or behaves so as to get the label. When the patient asked what the label was, the staff said the whole family must be called schizophrenic if one member is.

? Balaban: Is the purpose of this to test the treatment/method or to study the families of these patients?

Dr. Bowen: Both.

Dr. Zucker: Analytic terms or oral-anal orientation etc. might be used.

Dr. Bowen: Yes.

Dr. Zucker: In these terms oral and anal there is little about reference to communication. Could this be dangerous? (He went on to say something about amnesia in mother in child guidance clinics, in which she forgets the child's early years and also her own early years.) Is this because she is not differentiated yet from her own mother? Then, in therapy she can sometimes later remember.

4.

Dr. Brodey: We'll go into that later. A person remembers his own past history in relation to his own self image.

Question: Does patient know label?

Dr. Bowen: Yes.

Chatterton: Is this from the staff or from other sources?

Dr. Brodey: Families attend research meetings. The staff try to make themselves and their own positions as real and as clear as they can do.

Question: (?) Symonds: Are you trying to say that schizophrenia is suggested behavior?

Question: Who in the family or community labels the family as deviant?

Dr. Fleck: Isn't a step backward to use individual labels? Now there is need for study of intra-personal characteristics. Can't use simple labels for complicated interaction. Such words as spill, folie a famille, etc. represent efforts in this direction. The staff must present themselves as nakedly as they can. Staff group must learn to control own (something or other).

Rolfe: Bothered because people come because of having sick member. Therefore, how is it possible not to label?

Dr. Fleck: Challenges this. Family come but send one member to represent them.

Auster: Back to what is labeled psychotic. What determines how sick the individual will get before seeking help?

Dr. Fleck: Problem is more/not to get away from the label, but labels are not useful for groups.

Dr. Bowen: Families are told that we do not accept the problem as the individual's, but as the problem of the entire family. Families have responded. Why didn't someone say so before?

Chatterton: Someone else may be sicker than the "patient"?

Brody: This is not a representative sample, it's selected. There is not a large number of families at intake. Not much turnover.

Chatterton: Is the presenting problem the family or the sickness? (I'm not sure I copied this correctly.)

Basamania: This is not a service agency but a research hospital, therefore it's not like the intake in a service agency. All are referred by physicians.

Brodey: In the history taking carbons are used so the same history goes for all. Chief complaint of one is the some for all. Present illness—whole family involvement.

5.

George Olive: Is the family's isolation of themselves significant as a part of the study?

Brodey: Yes. They become welded into the group quickly.

Zucker: Some other study, I guess, found that either first generation Americans, with very close family ties or fourth and fifth generation families have this much isolation, and leak of family ties produces the isolation. (Again I'm not sure I have the idea straight.)

Dr. Brodey's Paper

A few introductory remarks. He recognizes that he has used bold strokes in his descriptions. He also acknowledges that there is a continuum between normal and pathological.

Dr. Freedman: Identifying himself as from a treatment home in Boston. The implications in delays in treatment. The patient is pulled out of treatment. The problem is not of one individual only. The child is constricted by the role the mother set for him. Questions why the patient stays home so long. Patient is excluded from certain functions of the family—kept in the back room—kept for other reasons. Family may remove the patient from the hospital. Why does the patient come in at a particular time? History taking does not get to the crucial relationship nor does the patient's therapy either. Setting up home treatment service—case finding public health problems, a whole family is seen with Miss Rolfe as social worker. They find difficulty in making family diagnosis. (From this hodgepodge of notes, I think, he was discussing his own work and his experiences in case finding and public health work, that the patient is often excluded from functions of the family, kept in the back room or kept home for other reasons, which may be the same reasons for which the family will eventually remove him from the hospital. I think he's raising questions about why does the patient come into the hospital at a particuar time? Why is treatment delayed? Until this time? How is the child restricted by the role the mother set?)

Zucker: Some work that is being done in Amsterdam. A team goes out to the home. They're on call for crisis, and they leave a member there at the family. Butler is now trying such an approach.

Satir: The role of the father is very much part of the symbiotic relationship with the mother. At times he goes along with the mother. At the point when the psychosis breaks out, he may be at odds with the mother. She gives a case. The father is a drunk and a gambler. The girl goes on a U.S.O. tour away from home. The mother then insists that the father stop gambling. The girl becomes ill. I'm not sure but what she gave other details, such as the mother having a hysterectomy; the girl having just finished high school, in this one; but if these crop up in a later case, than this isn't the one.

6.

Dr. Brodey: Dr. Bowen will discuss this in the afternoon. The role of the superrational and irrational in families. Sick behavior is denied or (Dr. Fleck interjects—is considered normal.)

Dr. Zucker: There is an adaptation to increments and we see the situation after many increments have been added.

Brodey: The family will say that everything has been normal up to this point, then there has been decompensation.

Zucker: Somewhere in the family is the assumption . . . (this I missed.) Woman's intuition is important in this culture because the woman chooses the husband and it is specific to this culture.

Dr. Fleck: This could be done in any culture. Refers to Spiegel and Kluekhelm study. How do various cultures make a psychotic? Diagnosis of psychosis may be the same, but the etiological or cultural background may vary. Again, I'm not sure I understand this comment.

Dr. Fleck to Dr. Freedman: You are after the most hopeless item of data. In our experience it's either accidental or not obtainable from the family any-way. They may give an explanation about why the patient comes in at this time, but it may irrelevant. Some extraneous force perhaps is impinging on the family but not necessarily from within; therapeutic or deteriorative. The patient is not isolated from the family. This is why the family ties to get the patient back. In some instances though, in state hospitals, where the equilib-rium has shifted and new equilibrium has become established in the absence of the patient; then the family cannot re-accept the patient.

Dr. Freedman: Could this be accidental? Have had difficulty determining when the patient became ill, or at least defined as schizophrenic.

Dr. Fleck: In one of our cases, a boy was considered by the mother sick because of a fire. Now she believes he remains sick because of what the hospital does to him.

Rosenblatt: Expressed interest in Brodey's observation, how when you are listening to the family, what they are doing or saying seems logical, until you begin to wonder why, and then it is bizarre. He describes a situation in which a child bursts into the office where he's seeing the mother, asking, "Is he a nice man?" and the mother says, "Does he look like one?" This is bizarre when looked at retrospectively.

Brodey: When the patient became ill is a sociological problem. The illness starts at no particular time, it's an interactional problem. Everyone has his own sense of reality. You see yours as the real one; the family's is the bizarre one. There's a disparity also between what the staff see and what the family report.

Rosenblatt: Such a response from a mother is not psychotic.

Long: How can the staff undercut the family's efforts to impose role of behavior on them? Is there group therapy of the staff?

7.

Brodey: As a continuum again—the staff became aware of it only when it gets to extreme. We do meet with all families and all staff sit down together, all try to observe interaction together.

Long: A girl in treatment at University Hospital after three years, says the staff do things to her. It's a question, how much of this is real.

Brodey: The projection becomes real. There's no way of controlling this very much.

Flecks: Before to a patient's mother who insisted that the boy must go to college to such an extent that by the end of the interview, Dr. Fleck would not have let the boy go to college, even if he'd been a super-student. He still had good reason for saying, No, but this was no longer what he was talking with at the end of the interview with the mother.

Zucker: The term "psychosis" has no real medical meaning. It was used in order to avoid the legal "insane."

Satir: Have yet to find a case involving schizophrenic member of the family
. . . (but I don't know what this means.) Patient's breakdown took place when
sister left for nurse's training. He graduated from high school, was appointed
to West Point. The father lost his job, at the same time, because of a heart
ailment. When you see what forces converge here you see that the boy did
not dare. He lost his sister, he could not dare to go along with his training.
Therefore, there is some reason to see why it becomes overt at this point.
Another factor here was the mother's menopause.

Dr. Fleck: These are more or less accidental but not in the sense that you can't
figure them out.

Satir: They're accidental when the developmental task becomes too much
in the face of these things. What were the mother's expectations of an adult
male in this case?

Rosenblatt to S. Fleck: Are you leading to the statement that it's the family
that has schizophrenia?

Rolfe: It's part of the pathology if the family cannot deal with regular developmental problems.

Zucker: The families are in a sense, standing still in time.

Brodey: Dr. Bowen will discuss this.

Alice R. Cornelison

8.

P.H.-DR. BOWEN'S PAPER

Dr. Fleck: We ought to get back to an abstract analysis of what went on.

Brodey: Contrasting the earlier and later periods, we see the mother attacks
the daughter, and the daughter counter-attacks. Only part of the personality is
available. It's interesting that as therapy progressed, there is more expression
outside of what is inside. You see, the therapists struggle to keep away from
the deciding role. When change comes about, the family members begin to
tell each other what they were doing. When the therapist moved out of the

situation, telling them it's your problem, then the family were able to work themselves at their own problem. He made a reference to Dr. Bowen's slip, in which Dr. Bowen said the father is talking to the father, rather than to the therapist.

Dr. Fleck: The mother's misunderstanding of the daughter's question, "May I have intercourse?" when she answers, "It's up to you to decide how often."

Dr. Bowen: The mother was making an effort and thought that this was the right course of action to take, even though she didn't believe in it. Dr. Bowen thought that this was correct for her, also.

Dr. Zucker: The mother was being a good little girl and also being the therapist when she says, "Don't bother me—don't wake me." Dr. Bowen made a response which I did not get.

Betty Basamania: Said there are no ground rules yet in the therapy with the family as a unit.

Long: The therapist is a particular-observer or eventually just as observer?

Dr. Bowen then drew Diagram #1 on the blackboard and explained the little wiggle as a narcissistic barrier between the parents. They would merge if they let go, but they control themselves by keeping a great distance. The parents can relate to the daughter, but not to each other. The mother in this case which he cited picked up and went forward. If the therapist is not structuring the therapy, the parents cannot deal with each other without great emotion.

Then he drew the second diagram and explains, he starts talking to her (see below):

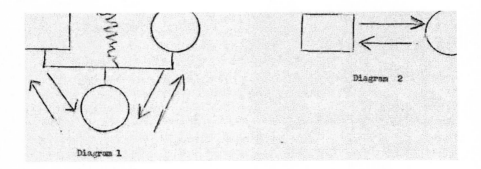

Diagram 1

Diagram 2

9.

Then to the air, then to the therapist.

Long: Is this interpreted?

Dr. Bowen: Yes.

Zucker: Tenderness seems to be missing in narcissistic parents. The mother marries in hope that she will get tenderness, but marries a man who cannot give it, repeating her childhood and into this situation, children cannot fit.

Dr. Bowen: The time the father was having the prostate operation was the time the mother moved.

Dr. Zucker: Don't you feel empathic with the mother here?

Dr. Bowen: Yes, but when you feel you want to applaud, you must watch yourself. If you start identifying or taking sides even in yourself, you had better hold counsel with yourself.

Question: Do you tell them about it when you feel this?

Dr. Bowen: You could in individual therapy.

Dr. Fleck: The therapist is also more vulnerable here than in individual therapy.

Dr. Bowen: This was started on the ward with four therapists. It helps but this is not easy either. Robert Dysinger was asked to sit in. Then he drew Diagram 3.

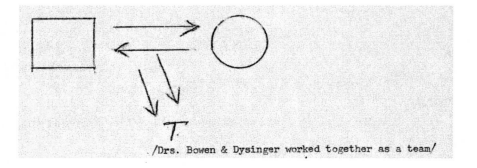

/Drs. Bowen & Dysinger worked together as a team/

First Bob Dysinger was outside the group, then after blowing up two families, it was decided that Dr. Bowen and Dr. Dysinger didn't understand their own relationship, and Dr. Bowen decided to go ahead alone.

Rosenblatt: What do you do when they talk to Dr. Bowen instead of to each other?

Dr. Bowen: (I'm not sure what he meant here.) I wrote—Go on free assoc. Stop resisting. (Perhaps he tells them to go on free associating and stop their resisting.)

Satir: Case represents an example of relating and appealing to whatever ego is there.

10.

Dr. Bowen: You said it beautifully. You usually can't do this with schizophrenics, but you can with the family there, because you do not have to be the mother.

Dr. Rose: You mention that the patient was in restraint, packs, etc. Who was responsible for this?

Dr. Bowen: I tried to have nothing to do with this. (This was a reference to a point this morning. The patient is brought to the hospital—it's when they can't stand it anymore.) Dr. Bowen did not want to be identified with putting the patient in the hospital.

Dr. Rose: I felt you were giving the family permission to hospitalize her.

Dr. Bowen: Yes.

Long: Commented on—Why did the mother make improvements—then as the girl got better, the mother got weaker. You see this in marital counseling.

Dr. Bowen: In an immature marriage, each parent must dominate or submit and as the family becomes more mature, each can do either—dominating or submitting without a problem. In these it's an awful problem. Then when you put a third family member in . . .

Long: But when one moves backward, he doesn't move so far.

Auster: Remarkable persistence of the mother in forcing the family into treatment. This is different from his own experience. The father's hospitalization here gave him legitimate dependency, so the mother was able to give up the demands of their own dependency. There is an impression that the mother was making conscious efforts, in spite of what she really felt. Usually the patient is in tune with what is really felt. How could the patient then respond to what the mother was saying.

Dr. Bowen: There are indications that the mother's move was related to the father's hospitalization; that is, for the prostatectomy, I think; but not to the daughter. But she said she would not elaborate. They talked about mutual feelings, but . . . (and, I think, this is a reference to the mother's talking one way about the patient's asking her mother if she could have intercourse. The mother's saying, Go ahead if you think it's the thing to do, in spite of the mother's feelings that she did not want her daughter to do it. Dr. Bowen went on to say that this was similar to a situation in therapy, when the therapist perhaps has an unconscious wish to baby the patient, but can still control the situation, and make the therapy work in spite of his own need.)

Long: The mother seems to be putting the therapist in the position of the father and taking strength from him.

Dr. Bowen: Can't say.

Dr. Fleck: The chances are that this woman had a passive father.

11.

Dr. Zucker: Perhaps the mother had to get rid of the girl before the father stood up for her too much.

Dr. Bowen: Regarding the father's bankruptcy, the attorneys wrote that the father had regressed and could not fulfill his obligations. The father started going bankrupt right after Dr. Bowen had told him he must assert himself.

Gliva: Didn't the daughter's response indicate a shift in the mother's unconscious?

Dr. Bowen: Think so, but has not thought in these terms.

Dr. Brodey: Drew the next diagram which I labeled #4

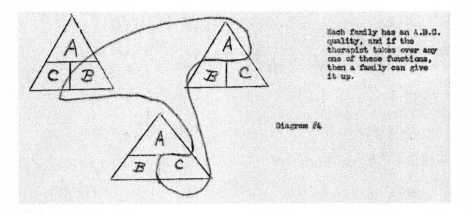

Each family has an A.B.C. quality, and if the therapist takes over any one of these functions, then a family can give it up.

Diagram #4

Dr. Fleck: A less sick patient can complain about the therapist's real inability to enter the situation.

Satir: Noting how parents got together at first—mostly drifting—trying to be a whole—the child upsets this. What was a blame situation becomes a seeking for wholeness. (I think she was saying here that the parents have a feeling of not being integrated selves and are seeking for this scene disrupts this, and when the situation is formulated in this way, it becomes apparent that it is not a situation in which the parents can be blamed for doing purposeful harm, but ought to be understood because they are seeking something they need for themselves.)

Rosenblatt: Is the situation similar when the impaired member is male?

Dr. Bowen: Has seen no great difference. The problem is, but none has appeared in the families studied.

Rosenblatt: Symbiosis might be stronger with a girl.

12.

Dr. Bowen: Three mother-daughter pairs were studied, in all. The family that has done the poorest has the greatest distance between the parents, which was covered up by tight formality. They were the most helpless people you could image. People in the hospital let down, become passive and do not move so fast. Dr. Bowen feels that in another family, where the differences between husband and wife were more overt, there was the best response to therapy.

Long: Why did you select young adults rather than children?

Dr. Bowen: Working eight years before with schizophrenics had been previous experience. (I've written after that note, pref. or spec; but I don't know what I meant.)

Dr. Fleck: Schizophrenia is bad enough. In childhood schizophrenia it's still more difficult to make it clear diagnosis. Also, most of the people interested in such studies are adult psychiatrists. (With us, dep. And I don't know what else I was going to say.)

Rosenblatt: Striking parallels between these and families of schizophrenic children. These mothers saw the child as images of themselves and could not stand it. There ensured an outbreak of pan hospitality.

Dr. Fleck: Marital partners who can't even fight anymore show much greater distance more remoteness.

Dr. Zucker: This is not peculiar to schizophrenics—enuretics, etc. may show some of these things.

Dr. Fleck: Doesn't agree. A schizophrenic is not so very basic. It is learned behavior—something about a basic personality problem. (My recording has lost the thread of the discussion here, I think, but I think it had something to do with whether or not schizophrenic was an organic or organic-like psychosis. I'm not sure.)

Dr. Bowen: There is the problem of differentiating the schizophrenia and the neurotic and (?) sense than what's normal . . . (I don't know what I meant there.)

Satir: People who come for analysis with "no need" show some pathology anyway.

Dr. Fleck: We have tested some so-called "normal" but what the tests show is pathology. How can we know what to look for? We have found borderline schizophrenic children who later develop—in the so-called normal families—who later developed serious problems, but they are still functioning in the community.

Dr. Bowen: There is a problem of diagnosis for the family. Can it be made in terms of functioning? How?

Long: Question of drugs and psychotherapy. How much Compazine was the patient getting?

13.

Dr. Bowen: She got loose from it, but Dr. Bowen doesn't know how. The mother used to grab her and make her take it. She probably went on it for about three months.

Long: Did you see a relation between the drug and what went on?

Dr. Bowen: Complacent patient on drugs did not respond to the mother's attack. (Something here I don't understand in my notes . . . something that a patient who can verbalize well on the drug; the patient says, she's lost herself, can't get motivation. Dr. Bowen has mixed feelings about drugs. Perhaps in this case it gave the family a chance to rest and to deal with the situation. The mothers in this study have demanded Thorazine. They gave it then, to the mothers to administer. Then decided against it because they wanted to work in a strictly psychotherapeutic way.)

Unknown questioner asked about follow-up.

Dr. Bowen: These are dead end patients. They have not been able to return a whole family to the community.

Long: You seem to feel that the family moved faster than the hospital—that this family moved faster than the hospitalized families. Does the family regress in the hospital?

Dr. Bowen: Yes.

Dr. Fleck: It's everybody's experience that once in a while you get a patient that you can treat outside in brief psychotherapy outside of the hospital. There's a money question. In a private hospital you often exhaust the family's funds in a year or two. The willingness of parents to sacrifice for the child plays into the malignancy. He cites a case of a resident who is mad at a father who would not mortgage his house for his daughter's therapy. Perhaps the daughter's relationship with the father would be improved if she knew her parents would not mortgage their lives for her.

Dr. Zucker: You must admire Dr. Bowen's ego strength. Look at the therapist's side of it.

Dr. Fleck: This resident would not be able to move realistically as Dr. Bowen.

Rose: The therapist sometimes gets the feeling that he's not important until you see a man such as this, who becomes bankrupt in order to get even with Dr. Bowen for suggesting that he be more assertive.

Unknown Questioner: Can you evaluate the ability of the family to move into this situation, when they have had previous contact with psychiatrists or social workers? Does the previous contact, in other words, color their response to this situation?

Dr. Fleck: Something about difficulty in himself to induce people to take the step. (Here I felt Dr. Fleck did not understand the question as asked. Someone picked it up sometime later. I lost the discussion at the point, again . . .)

14.

Dr. Bowen: The girl had a lot of strength—more than others. She had been Phi Beta Kappa at college. Many of the people who come have been in treatment before. We have been finding in all sorts of practice that we have more and more with experience with therapy.

Dr. Fleck: We could duplicate this situation with one in which only the patient was hospitalized. The parents were seen separately. The patient is doing well but another child has had to have treatment, so it's possible that the problem was simply transferred to the other child.

Dr. Bowen: Once you can get the parents to be themselves without doubt or apology they can still do the craziest things, but the patient responds very well. The problem is how to keep them facing anxiety without having to leave. He cited a case. The mother goes to Florida to be mothered by a fifteen-year-old normal daughter. The father mothers the patient for a while, then goes down to Florida and insists upon his authority. Cuts willow sticks and threatens the 15 year old daughter, I think, with these . . . maybe the mother, I'm not sure whom he threatened. But this was crazy behavior and yet the kids responded well to it. Kids have trouble responding to a theoretical system imposed on them by parents who don't really have a feeling for what they are doing.

Zucker: Young children can sense what is going on, but they are looking in the judgment about it and respond, therefore, instead to what they hear and see.

Dr. Fleck: Parents of artistic children seem similar. Parents are intelligent, they are following books, over-educated.

Satir: How are the siblings related to the basic triangle.

Dr. Bowen: Cites Benedict, Mahler, Reichert and Tillum and Lidz—on Symbiosis Concept of narcissism—more in Dr. Brodey's idea. Dr. Bowen is not clear about this or about ego psychology. Observations support some of this that the mother in her isolation has an intense relationship with a child; that it is shifted to successive children; from boys to girls; from girls to boy. A boy could be the support—or need women to understand them—could be the reasons.

Long: Is the essential component the support that the mother gets or her need to project on the child her own pathological conflicts.

Dr. Fleck: It's not that simple. The child sops up anxiety of the mother or of the father. With a sibling there is the effectiveness, etc. In case of twins that we studied different roles were assigned to them by the mother; one masculine and no feminine, so the two had different types of homosexual problems.

Unknown Questioner: You mentioned the passivity of hospitalized families. Are gyn or g.u. problems more likely to occur in hospitalized families.

Dr. Bowen: Dr. Robert Dysinger took care of the medical problems because it got too complicated having outside internists come in.

15.

Dr. Dysinger: We have seen long neglected medical problems finally ended to real assessment. Four parents had difficulty dealing with actual physical things. They must relate all things to the group, so they would try to get around this by having medical problems and elaborating on them; having therefore, a private relationship with a doctor. They were emotionally determined somatic reactions—hives—many of them. (I think, Dr. Bowen spoke up here, and said something about three findings in which there were these gyn. Or gu. Difficulties in either or both parents.)

Freedman: (? Not sure it was he?) He is pleased to hear that the parents are getting more humane treatment. The total involvement relieves them of blame. Heretofore, therapists have been isolated to blame the child's lack of progress on the parents.

Dr. Zucker: You see as you work more in this that one does not judge illness.

Oliva: Didn't people come in the first place to be helped to be themselves? (Referring back to an earlier point of Dr. Bowen's.)

Dr. Bowen: Yes, but it's hard to give up the old way of functioning.

Dr. Zucker: You could say that they come because of what they think they should be, rather than what they are.

Satir: It's a mistake to think of people as having had help before. It may take time to get across to them that you have a different expectation.

Blair: The distant parent had a narcissistic expectation for himself and for the child. In treatment he learns to give this up.

Unknown Questioner: Wouldn't the outlook be more promising with younger families?

Dr. Bowen: We would be in favor of working more and more with families together. Started this to keep down the fire in the environment, then it was so successful—we gave up the other ways of treating.

Mark: Has been relating this work with her own to the aged. Grown children together with an elderly parent might benefit from discussing the problem all in a group. She feels this applies to any age group.

Dr. Bowen: Has thought of this in children planning for an aging parent. They might all get out their resentments and hostilities in one explosion and then get to work from there. At least, this is the impression I got from what I thought he meant.

Unknown Questioner: Is there an even deeper and tighter symbiosis between husband and wife. Where they will not let you touch this, except through the children? Symbiosis perhaps becomes alive with the child—as an atom is split off. Is the relationship between the parents not touched?

Dr. Bowen: He believes the original symbiosis—that between the parents—is touched. The father asserts himself. The mother becomes anxious. If the Father can keep his stand then the mother becomes more objective, then she becomes very calm. There is a very close relationship to each other, almost like a honeymoon. The child then, becomes more psychotic in order to get the mother back.

16.

Dr. Fleck: Our patient (referring to Jeff) did not pull together when his parents came apart. He did fall apart when they came together, which lasted for a few months. Perhaps he has not pulled together again because the mother has remained distant. Another parental relationship can continue at the expense of the child. There can be a rivalry between parent and child as with Don B. in which the father left home leaving the mother and the child together most of the time but was very rivalrous with the child when he was around.

Summary of the Discussion

The discussion began with preliminary questions about the setting, selection of patients, how the patients and families felt about the project, about coming into the hospital, what were the charges for them, what kind of physical set-up was provided, etc. Then the question of diagnosis arose and whether one is attached to the entire family or not. I am not sure it is clear in the dictated discussion but I felt that it came out quite clearly that Dr. Bowen wanted to avoid a labeling of the patient as schizophrenic and wanted to, if using any label at all, to attach it to the entire family.

The discussion then shifted to the family's interactions with each other, whether they speak together or isolated from each other, can see each other's problems, if not their own, etc. A few theoretical questions were asked about whether these were multi-generation problems, whether significant relatives, who might make their homes with the family, are included in the study such as a grandmother etc. The question also arose as to what the diagnosis means to the family. Dr. Bowen apparently felt that they would live up to any label that was suggested for them and Dr. Brody felt that these people were particularly sensitive to what they felt was expected of them, and would behave accordingly. There was other theoretical discussion about labels, analytic terms, oral, anal, etc. The point was brought out that the families attend the research meetings and the staff tried to participate as openly as they expect the family to do. There was considerable discussion about the importance, or the need for labels to describe interaction among people rather than labeling people as if their problems were those of single unattached individuals.

The discussion then reverted to intake and selection of family's history again.

Discussion after Dr. Brodey's Paper

There was discussion about why the patient stays at home, why the patient comes into the hospital when he does, what this has to do with the role of the father and with the symbiotic relationship with the mother etc. Some of this was referred to Dr. Bowen's paper in the afternoon, and Dr. Zucker felt that there was an adaptation to increments until the thing gets too much. Dr. Fleck thought that the reason for admission could not really be determined—that is, the real reason—that many accidental factors converged. The discussion continued about when the illness starts, when it is recognizable, how the family can live with it, without recognizing it, how sometimes, there is the appearance of logic in a very illogical and irrational interchanges, so that it might conceivably go unnoticed. And with a continuum, one may become aware only when an extreme is approached. There was further discussion of the point that Dr. Brody had made that the things the family member projects may become real because the staff members may be provoked into assuming the roles attributed to them. Satir questioned whether Dr. Fleck's point about the factors causing the hospitalization being accidental. She considered that they were difficulties in meeting developmental problems which are problems of ordinary development, but many difficulties may converge at one time. And someone thought that it was part of the pathology of the family that they were not able to deal with these regular developmental problems.

Afternoon Session—Dr. Bowen

Dr. Brodey commented on the earlier and later periods in the therapy, when the therapist was at first intervening more actively; then stepping back and telling the family that it was their problem—they would have to decide. Dr. Fleck called attention to the mother's misunderstanding of the daughter's question and distorting it somewhat in her answer, that is, when the daughter asked, "May I have intercourse?" The mother says, "It's up to you to decide how often." And Dr. Bowen felt that this was an effort in the right direction, but conceded that the mother did not agree, really basically, with what she was doing. She felt that it was necessary for her to do it, but difficult because it was in opposition to her code of behavior. Dr. Zucker called attention to the fact that the mother was being a good little girl and also was being the therapist. (I thought this was an important point—that the mother was trying to please the therapist and also trying to identify with him.) Then there was comment about the parents being able to relate to the daughter but not to each other and whether or not the therapist can structure the therapy, and how the parents can deal with the stress of the emotion when brought out when they must deal with each other. There was some talk about the parents' needs and disappointments in their marriage. Dr. Bowen cautioned against the therapist's wanting to applaud action of one or another member of the family, or to take sides, and the difficulties which were introduced when another therapist joined the treatment situation, with the two therapists not fully understanding their relationship with each to immature her. Then, more discussion of the effort to relate and appeal to whatever go strength is present in the family.

The importance of the therapist remaining neutral. The difficulties that the parents in an immature marriage have in resolving their problems relating to dominating and submitting, either or both of which may be required of them but which they are not able to deal with without conflict. The question was raised about whether the mother's effort to express to her daughter an attitude which she did not really feel could be successful and Dr. Bowen indicated that sometime the therapist must do such also, and can be in control and can be successful. There was talk about the relationship between the mother's move forward and the father's hospitalization with a prostate, and the prevalence of gyn. and gu. problems in these families. There was more discussion of the therapist's role in the situation, whether the mother then, puts the therapist in the position of a strong father and takes strength from him. There was also discussion of the father's becoming bankrupt immediately after Dr. Bowen told him he must assert himself with the mother. And whether the fact that the daughter responded to the mother's behavior indicated a real shift in the mother's unconscious. Also to what extent does the therapist take over certain roles in the family relieving the family of the need to fill these functions and freeing them to explore other avenues, perhaps of problem-solving. And the discussion gradually took the turn of giving more recognition to the parents as people who have problems of their own, and perhaps have been in need of help for some time on their own. Then more questions about selection of patients, about symbiosis, what are normal families, what does normal functioning mean, perhaps in spite of pathology. Questions about the use of drugs. Again, discussion of the therapist's role the importance of the position the therapist assumes in the family, what strengths there are to work with? Dr. Bowen made the point—I guess, made in his paper also, that the parents' sureness of themselves may be almost more important that what they do. If they are filled with doubts and apologies, the patient resets adversely; whereas, if they feel sure of themselves, they can behave in very bizarre ways without alarming or disturbing the patient, or without upsetting the patient. Then, there was much talk about narcissism, about the part of the child in evoking certain behavior from the parents, about the growing passivity in the families which have been admitted to the hospital, as contrasted with those who remain on the outside, and the discussion ended with suggestions about other applications for this method and further means for developing it. Work with aged, work with younger families, perhaps being more hopeful, and again the question of symbiosis and whether that between husband and wife might not be the primary one.

5

The 1959 Family as a Unit of Study and Treatment Workshop

INTRODUCTION

While this workshop was given during the last year of the project, the papers were not published until 1961. Bowen's paper on Family Psychotherapy is also a chapter in *Family Therapy in Clinical Practice*. However, the introduction to this article is not published in his book.

Bowen's introduction to the research project provides a useful summary. He makes it clear that the material for the workshop was derived from a research project where parents and their schizophrenic children lived on a live-in research unit for observation and treatment.

The theoretical orientation "the family as the unit of illness" regarded the psychosis in the patient as a symptom of an active process that involved the entire family. The treatment approach "the family as the unit of treatment" was a method of psychotherapy in which all family members attended psychotherapy hours together (Bowen, 1961, p. 40).

Of further interest in the introduction about the research project is Bowen's discussion about the specific number of families who participated in the project. The exact number of participants is difficult to find. Bowen states there were 18 family units involved in the Family Research Study. This included three mother-daughter dyads from the first year; two of these continued in the study after the first year when the orientation changed to a "family unit" focus. By today's standards of length of care, it is amazing that one of the mother-patient families lived in the project for 25 months and another for 35 months. Additionally, there were seven families with parents, patient, and normal siblings who lived "in residence" for an average length of stay of just under one year. It was these seven families that formed the basis of the study.

In addition, there were 8 outpatient families of parents, patient, and siblings who were seen for over 30 months, and an additional 12 families who were evaluated as outpatients. However, Basamania (1961, p. 75) noted there were only eleven families in the project. Thus, the sample size of the project needs clarification.

Dr. Bowen introduces all the papers in the workshop. He notes that family psychotherapy and the concept of the family as emotional units are "interwoven." The second paper is by Robert Dysinger, M.D. It was Dr. Dysinger who served in the dual roles of family psychotherapist and family physician for the project families during the last three years of the research. This paper illustrates the important but often overlooked relationship between family emotional processes and somatic illness.

The third paper, by Warren Brodey, M.D., uses a psychoanalytic orientation and discusses "perceptual distortions between family members" (Bowen, 1961, p. 42). The fourth and last paper is by Betty Basamania, MSS, a clinical social worker in the project. Like the other professional staff, her "job description" changed significantly from the familiar orientation of individual psychotherapist to the new role of family psychotherapist. Her paper describes this change from the perspective of social casework, the term used at that time. The four papers are important summaries of the Family Study Project by the primary participants in the research. The following section will include an overview of each paper.

Bowen's paper on Family Psychotherapy is well known. He considered it important enough to include it as chapter 5 in his classic text *Family Therapy in Clinical Practice*. Bowen's version of family psychotherapy is perhaps the only type of family therapy based on research and theoretical principles. One central principle is that the family is viewed as an emotional unit. The theoretical efforts were directed to the "family oneness" rather than "emotional oneness" of the mother-daughter dyads.

Bowen describes a number of steps required in the shift from the individual. First, there was the ability to think in terms of the family unit rather than an individual with symptoms. Second, and more difficult, were the abilities to relate to the family, and to treat the family therapeutically. These were not easy steps.

Another important aspect of Bowen's paper is the issue of defining "functional helplessness" and the importance of finding a family leader.

In my opinion these families are not really helpless. They are functionally helpless. The parents are adequate, resourceful people in their outside relationships. It is in relationship to each other that they become functionally helpless. When the family is able to be a contained unit, and there is a family leader with motivation to define the problem and to back his own convictions in taking appropriate action, the family can change from a directionless, anxiety-ridden, floundering unit, to a more resourceful organism with a problem to be solved. (Bowen, 1961, p. 56)

The second paper, written by Robert Dysinger, M.D., was called "A Family Perspective on the Diagnosis of Individual Members." It was Dr. Dysinger who provided medical consultation to the family members in the study. His focus was on the emotional and physical functioning in the project families. An important pattern emerged where the family members were found to "participate in an intense emotional process with one another in which health issues are consistently involved" (Dysinger, 1961, p. 62). There was also a blurring between facts and feelings; "anxiety is regularly regarded as evidence of some kind of disease" (Dysinger, 1961, p. 63).

Another pattern noted by Dysinger was that mothers in the project assumed the role of "family diagnostician," a position supported by the fathers. The symptomatic child also participated with the parents: "The intense involvement about health matters in the mother-father-child group is most openly active with respect to the child" (Dysinger, 1961, p. 64). The parents treat the child as if they were quite fragile. All family members were also overinvolved with each other. Dysinger viewed physical health complaints at the family level. In addition, he concluded that parental emotional problems were played out in the health arena of the child who was the identified patient. Dysinger's work in this area is important but is often overshadowed by other major Family Study Project findings.

The title of Dr. Warren Brodey's paper, *Image, Object and Narcissistic Relationships* seems out of place given the overall focus of the Family Study Project. In the *Image, Object and Narcissistic Relationships* paper he describes how the concepts of narcissistic, image, and object relationships apply to project families. A pattern of relating was apparent and described as "a relationship with a projected or distanced part of self as mirrored in the behavior of another" (Brodey, 1961, p. 71). Seeing the families as a single organism, Brodey describes how these concepts apply to families with a schizophrenic child.

The last paper in the workshop was by Betty Basamania, MSS, the clinical social worker in the project. Her overall summary of the project is as follows:

The research project offered an apt framework for the study of the emotional life of the family unit and for the development of an approach to the unit that involved the entire family. The theoretical orientation regarded the schizophrenic problem as part of a process that involved the entire family. Systematic observations of family units were consistent with this hypothesis, and treatment, based upon these observations, was adapted to the family unit. (Basamania, 1961, p. 74)

Her perspective is from a social casework approach to the family and how that may contribute to family diagnosis and treatment. Basamania is clear that "the observations were made as a result of seeing the family as a unit, and would have been much less clear, if not obscured, if family members had been seen individually" (75). She grouped her observations in two categories. First, there were interconnected personality problems between family members, and second, problematic family interactions. Basamania found that when families are seen together, the family members decrease involvement with each other and look to "experts" to recommend solutions.

In summarizing the therapy accomplished in the project, Basamania noted a distinct change in the traditional therapeutic relationship. That is, "the therapist could not establish one-to-one relationships with individual members in the family unit and have therapy effective" (82). With family psychotherapy, a great deal of self-awareness is required in order to preserve objectivity: "Transference and counter-transference are present in therapy with the family unit but can be diluted" (83). The word "diluted" is interesting and descriptive.

In the last section on the importance of the project for social work, Basamania makes several observations. First, with family psychotherapy, the patient's original family relationships were maintained. Second, projection of family problems to psychotic patients had not been widely reported although it was a common finding with less intense problems. Lastly, the method of family psychotherapy eliminated common clinical decisions such as which family members are seen in therapy, and which therapist should see which family member.

The Family as a Unit of Study & Treatment Workshop, 1959
The Family as the Unit of Study and Treatment Workshop, 1959
Stephen Fleck, M.D. Chairman*

1. Family Psychotherapy
Murray Bowen, M.D.
*Associate Professor of Clinical Psychiatry, Georgetown University
School of Medicine, Washington, D.C.*
*Medical Director, Yale Psychiatric Institute, New Haven, Connecticut.
Formerly Chief, Family Study Section, Clinical Investigations, National Institute of Mental Health, Bethesda, Maryland.

The Research Project

The resource material for this workshop comes from a research project in which normal parents and their adult schizophrenic offspring lived together on a psychiatric ward of a research center in a continuing "in residence" observation and treatment situation. The theoretical orientation "the family as the unit of illness" regarded the psychosis in the patient as a symptom of an active process that involved the entire family. The treatment approach "the family as the unit of treatment" was a method of psychotherapy in which all family members attended all the psychotherapy hours together.

Certain important background information about the project will be summarized briefly in this introduction. The project was started in 1954 and terminated at the end of 1958. The study was first focused on the mother-patient relationship. Three mothers lived on the ward with the patients. Each mother and each patient had individual psychotherapy. The "living together" situation provided a new area of observational data that had not been anticipated from previous work with mothers and patients individually. This data led to the formulation of the "family unit" hypothesis that was instituted at the end of the first year. The psychosis in the patient was then seen as a single manifestation of the total family problem. The research plan was changed to admit families so that the entire family unit could live together on the ward. The psychotherapy was then directed at the family unit, rather than to individuals in the family.

A total of 18 families[1] participated in the study. This included the 3 mother-patient families from the individual phase. Two of the mother-patient-families continued to participate after the change to the "family unit" orientation. One of the mother-patient families lived on the ward for 25 months and the other for 35 months. There were 7 families with fathers, mothers, patients and normal siblings who lived "in residence" as long as 33 months and whose average participation was a few days under 12 months. These 7 families were the center point of the project. They provided observational data that made it possible to further define the hypothesis, and the psychotherapeutic data that made it possible to work out details of family psychotherapy. After the family psychotherapy was defined as a workable structure, there were 8 families with fathers, mothers and psychotic patients who were treated in outpatient family psychotherapy for periods as long as 30 months. An additional 12 families were studied in detailed outpatient evaluation. These families provided valuable supplemental data, but since they were not part of the family psychotherapy effort, they were not included in the research study.

A number of practical changes were involved in adapting the "family unit" operation to the ward setting. The ward could accommodate two or three families at a time, depending on the size of the families. Small families were chosen in order to accommodate as many as possible. The ward milieu was structured so that crucial elements of the family unit could be maintained in the living-together situation. The parents were required to assume the principal responsibility for the care of their psychotic offspring.

The nursing staff functioned more to help the parents than to assume direct responsibility for the patients. One parent was free to continue regular employment as long as the other parent remained with the patient and both parents could attend the daily family psychotherapy hours. Both parents could leave together by making arrangements with the nursing staff to "sit" with the patient. Parents could take the patients on outside trips provided they could handle the situation responsibly.

This long-term view of the families as they lived, ate, worked and played together during periods of calmness and crisis, periods of family success and family failure, and periods of serious family illness provided a "talking and action" view of the families that has not been equaled by any other situation in our experience. Also to be stressed is the fact that the staff was in a therapeutic position to the families. The psychotherapist, in a helping relationship, had access to an area of communication and data that is not available to the "objective observer" relationship.

The four papers of this workshop will deal with different facets of the same project. The authors have worked together as a clinical research team. Each will present material from an area of personal interest and clinical experience.

The paper on "Family Psychotherapy" by Dr. Murray Bowen is first because it includes a description of the theoretical premise that is the cornerstone on which the entire research and clinical operation was based. It is necessary that it be presented with family psychotherapy because the two are interwoven and each has contributed to the other.

In the second paper Dr. Robert Dysinger will present some observations from his experience as a family psychotherapist and also as family physician from the in-residence families. In our initial research design, somatic illness was handled as a phenomenon isolated from emotional problems. It was treated by an internist from another part of the hospital. In the second year the treatment of somatic illness was integrated with the psychotherapy. The integration effort went more toward achieving emotional objectivity as family physician than to achieving greater objectivity in the psychotherapy. The family physician found that he was practicing a kind of general medicine quite different, in many ways, from generally accepted practices.

In the third paper Dr. Warren Brodey, the "Mayor" of the family research community, will present a conceptual viewpoint developed to understand the details of the all-pervading perceptual distortions between family members. He uses a somewhat different frame of references than is used in the other papers.

Mrs. Betty Basamania, the psychiatric social worker on the research team, presents the fourth paper. Her function in the clinical operation was well defined when she had individual relationships with various family members.

After the change to the "family unit" orientation her clinical function was much less clear. In the course of the project her main clinical function came to be that of assistant family psychotherapist. In her effort to define her own role in the project, she has been particularly interested in the contributions and implications of the "family unit" approach to social casework. In her paper she will present an over-all view of the "family unit" approach with special emphasis on inferences for social casework. She covers some of the material that is also in the other papers but she has attempted to present it from a casework orientation.

Family Psychotherapy

The family psychotherapy for this research project was developed directly from the theoretical premise "the family as the unit of illness." Some knowledge of the theoretical premise is crucial to a clear understanding of the therapeutic approach. I shall deal first with the theoretical premise "the family as the unit of illness," and then with the psychotherapeutic approach "the family as the unit of treatment."

The development of the theoretical premise, presented in detail in other papers (1, 2, 3), will be summarized briefly. The first working hypothesis for the project was developed from previous experience in psychoanalytic psychotherapy with schizophrenic patients and with their parents. Improvement had been more consistent in the patients whose parents were also in psychotherapeutic relationships. Schizophrenia was regarded as a psychopathological entity within the person of the patient, which had been influenced to a principal degree by the child's early relationship with the mother. The basic character problem, on which psychotic symptoms were later super imposed, was considered to be an unresolved symbiotic attachment to the mother. The symbiotic attachment was regarded as an arrest in the normal psychological growth process between mother and child, which was initially neither wanted and against which both had struggled unsuccessfully over the years. This latter point was important. When the hypothesis avoided "blaming" the mothers, new theoretical and clinical flexibilities became possible. I believe "blaming" is inherently present, no matter how much it is toned down or denied, in any theory that views one person as "causal" to the problem in another. The hypothesis further postulated that mother and patient could begin to grow toward differentiation from each other with individual psychotherapy for both.

The research plan in the first year provided for mothers and patients to live together on the ward, for staff persons to interfere as little as possible in the relationship problems between the two, and for each to have psychotherapy.

The working hypothesis, formulated from experience with mothers and patients individually, had accurately predicted the way each would relate to the other as individuals. It did not predict, not even consider, a large area of observations that emerged from the living-together situation. The "emotional oneness" between mother and patient was more intense than expected. The oneness was so close that each could accurately know the other's feelings, thoughts and dreams in a sense they could "feel for each other," or even "be for each other." There were definite characteristics to the way the "oneness" related to fathers or other outside figures. This emotional oneness is quite different from the emotional separateness between the mothers and their normal children. There were repeated observations to suggest that the mother-patient oneness extended beyond the mother and patient to involve the father and other family members. The mothers and patients used individual psychotherapy more to restore harmony to the oneness that to differentiate from each other.

With the change to the family unit hypothesis, the focus was on the "family oneness" rather than on individuals. At that point we could have kept the familiar individual orientation and focused on characteristics of individual relationships, but we had the research facility to make an exploration into the different way of thinking, and there were observations to support the "family unit" hypothesis as a profitable way to approach the problem. The hypothesis was changed to regard the psychosis as a symptom of an active process that involved the entire family. Just as a generalized physical illness can focus in one organ, so schizophrenia was seen as a generalized family problem which disabled one member of the family organism. The research plan was changed to admit new families in which fathers, mothers, patients and normal siblings could live together on the ward. The research design was adapted to the family unit instead of the individual. For instance, the ward milieu was adapted for family activity rather than individual activity, and the staff attempted to think in terms of the family unit rather than the individual. The psychotherapy was changed to "family as the unit of treatment" approach.

The theoretical concept "the family as the unit of illness" is basic to every aspect of the research and clinical operation. It is the theoretical foundation from which psychotherapy was developed as a logical orderly system. The terms "family as a unit" and "family unit" are used as short forms of "the family as the unit of illness." On one level this concept appears so simple and obvious that it hardly deserves second mention. On another level, the concept is subtle and complex, with far-reaching implications that involve a major shift in the way man thinks about himself and illness, and in the theory shift in the way man thinks about himself and illness, and in the theory and practice of medicine. In an effort to communicate as clearly as possible about the concept, I shall describe some of the experiences of the staff in shifting from the individual to the family unit orientation.

The staff experienced three main levels of awareness of the family unit concept. The first was the level of intellectual awareness. It was relatively easy to understand the concept intellectually.

The second was the level of clinical awareness. It was infinitely more complex to put the concept into clinical operation than to understand it intellectually. First it was necessary to further clarify and define our own thinking. All existing theories, terminology, literature, teaching, the rules of society that deal with sick people, and the rules and principles that deal with the practice of medicine, are based on the familiar individual orientation. It was hard for the staff to give up this "second nature" way of thinking. Then came the problem of operation in a medical center which regarded "the individual as the unit of illness." The individual orientation in medicine is strict. It requires that the individual be called "patient" and that individual pathology be defined with tests and labeled with a "diagnosis." Failure to focus on the individual can be regarded as medical irresponsibility. Our problem was to find a way to operate a "family unit" project in an institution with an individual orientation. Our research center permitted a "For Research Study Only" diagnosis label. In general, the minimal individual requirements of the center were met, but within the research ward the use of "diagnoses" and the term "patient" was avoided. The same problem has come up in our writing. It becomes so complicated to avoid terms such as "patient" and "schizophrenia" that we have temporarily resolved the dilemma by sparing use of familiar terms. In the course of implementing the family unit concept into the clinical operation, we came to "know" the concept in a way that was quite different from the intellectual awareness.

The third level was that of emotional awareness. There was a definite process in changing from emotional identifications with the individual to an emotional awareness of the family unit. The first emotional reaction in a new staff member was usually over identification with one family member, usually the patient, and anger at the family member most involved with the patient, usually the mother. Family members work constantly to get staff members to support their individual viewpoints. The second emotional reaction was usually that of alternating over involvements, first with one, and then with another family member. Gradually there would come an emotional detachment from the stressful over involvements and a beginning capacity to become aware of the over-all family problem.

As I see it, the theoretical focus on the family unit, plus the constant daily contact with the living together situation, set the stage for this automatic detachment from the individual and the growing emotional awareness of the family. The detachment proceeded most rapidly in those who had the best control over countertransference over involvement. Some staff members were never free of over involvements with one family member and angers at other family members. It is essential that the family psychotherapist relate himself to the family and that he avoid over involvement with the individual. There are constant forces within the family and within himself to cause him to revert to the familiar individual orientation. When anxiety is high, the family members exert more pressure for individual relationships. When the therapist is anxious, he is more likely to respond with his second nature individual orientation that "feels right." I found that the use of terms associated with the individual orientation was sufficient stimulus to cause me to revert to individual thinking. I was responsible for the family psychotherapy. In an effort to maintain a family unit orientation, I avoided the use of many familiar psychiatric terms associated with the individual and forced myself to use simple descriptive terms. Other staff members have been freer to use familiar terms.

Early in the study we used a term which was discarded because it has certain inaccuracies, but it does convey a fairly clear notion of the hypothesized psychological unity in the family. The term *undifferentiated family ego mass* suggests a central family oneness. Some siblings are able to achieve almost complete differentiation from the family while others achieve less. The one who becomes psychotic is an example of one who achieves little differentiation. On one level each family member is an individual, but on a deeper level the central family group is as one. Our study was directed at the "undifferentiated family ego mass" beneath the individuals. In the literature the concept that appears to be closest to our family unit idea was presented by Richardson in Patients Have Families (4). He did not develop his concept as specifically as we have done, but one section of his book is headed "The family as the Unit of Illness" and another "The Family as a Unit of Treatment." With the increasing number of family research studies, terms such as "family unit" and "family as a unit" have become commonplace. Most investigators have used theoretical thinking based on individual theory, and "family unit" terms that refer in a nonspecific way to a group of individual family members. According to our hypothesis this would be a "family group" rather than a "family unit." The term "family psychotherapy" is also used frequently. We have used the term to refer to psychotherapy directed at the hypothesized emotional oneness within the family. According to our hypothesis, a psychotherapy based on individual theory and directed to a group of individuals in the same family would be "family group psychotherapy," which is quite different from the method "family psychotherapy" as presented here.

In an effort to remove the psychotherapy from the status of an empirical trial-and-effort method, it was incorporated into the research hypothesis so that the hypothesis determined the course of the psychotherapy and psychotherapy observations could be used to change the hypothesis. There were three main steps in adapting the hypothesis to the clinical operation. Each step had its own unique resistances. The first was to think in terms of the family unit rather than the individual. This step was incorporated into the hypothesis. Resistance to this was within the staff. It was difficult to give up "second nature" individual thinking. The second step was to relate to the family unit rather than to individuals. This step was incorporated into the research design. Resistance was both in the staff and in the families. In periods of high anxiety, the tendency to revert to the individual orientation was present both in families and in the staff. The third step was to treat the family psychotherapeutically as a single organism. This step was incorporated into the research as "family psychotherapy." Obviously it was necessary to first think of the family as a unit and to be reasonably successful at relating to the family unit before it was possible to treat the family as a unit.

Now to a consideration of the way the family psychotherapy was integrated into the total research plan. The first step was to state the hypothesis in great detail.[2] Every possible clinical situation was anticipated, explained according to the hypothesis, and recorded as predictions to be checked against clinical observations. The working hypothesis was thus a theoretical blueprint which postulated the origin, development and clinical characteristics of family problem, which served as a basis for knowing the clinical management before a clinical situation arose, and which predicted clinical response in family psychotherapy. This corresponds to the thinking step outlined above. The second step was the development of research design through which the working hypothesis could be put into clinical operation. The ward milieu was changed to fit the hypothesis as nearly as possible. For example, occupational therapy was planned for the family unit instead of the individual. This step corresponded to the relating step outlined above. The third step was the development of a psychotherapy consistent with the hypothesis.

Thus the entire operation came under the direction of the working hypothesis. Clinical predictions came to have great use. There were constant checks between predictions and actual observations. There were areas in which the predictions were amazingly accurate, and others with great inconsistency. The area of inconsistency then became areas for special study. Eventually, when there were sufficient clinical observations to support a change, the working hypothesis was reformulated, the research design and the psychotherapy modified to conform to the reformulated hypothesis, and new predictions made. In this way the psychotherapy was linked point by point with the hypothesis, and observations that recurred consistently in psychotherapy could eventually become the basis of a change in the hypothesis. It was possible at any time to make changes in psychotherapy but only after it was possible to reformulate the hypothesis and to make the changes on the basis of theory, rather than make changes in clinical emergencies that were based on "clinical judgment" or "feelings." The working hypothesis, which is also our current theoretical concept of schizophrenia, has been presented in detail in another paper (3).

There is a wealth of dramatic clinical observations in a project such as this. The main problem is selecting and classifying data. I have focused on broad patterns of behavior rather than detail, and specifically on broad patterns present in all the families. There are a number of these which have been incorporated into the working hypothesis, which then served as the basis for modification of the psychotherapy. These relationship patterns have been described in other papers (3, 5, 6), but they have played such an important part in the development of the psychotherapy that it is necessary to summarize some of them here.

Family members are quite different in their outside business and social relationships than in those within the family. It is striking to see a father who functions successfully and decisively in business but who, in relation to the mother, becomes unsure, compromising and paralyzed by indecision. In all the families there has been emotional distance between the parents which we have called the "emotional divorce." At one extreme were the parents with a calm controlled distance from each other. The parents had few over-disagreements and they saw the marriage as ideal. The marriages had the form and content of closeness in that they went through the actions of closeness and used terms of endearment associated with closeness, but emotion was obliterated. Neither husband nor wife could communicate inner thoughts, fantasies or feelings to each other, although both could communicate thoughts and feelings to others. At the other extreme were parents who fought and argued in their brief periods of closeness and who spent most of their time in a "cold war" distance from each other. Most of the parents maintained the distance with varying combinations of calm control and overt disagreement.

Both parents are equally immature. In outside relationships both could cover up the immaturity with facades of maturity. In their relationship with each other, especially when they attempted to function together as a team, one would immediately become the adequate or overstrong one and the other the inadequate or helpless one. Neither could function in the midground between these two extremes. Either could function in either position, depending on the situation. Overadequate fathers were cruel and authoritative and inadequate mothers were helpless and complaining. Overadequate mothers were dominating and bossy and inadequate fathers were passive and compliant.

We have called this the "overadequate-inadequate reciprocity." The one who makes a decision for the two of them immediately becomes the overadequate one who is seen as "dominating" the other, who is "forced into submission." When neither will immediately "give in" they fight and argue. Neither wants the responsibility of "dominating," the anxiety of "submitting," nor the discomfort of fighting. The emotional divorce is a mechanism to make the relationship more comfortable. They keep the distance, avoid teamwork decisions, seek individual activities and share inner thoughts and feelings with relatives, friends, children or other outside figures. As the years pass, the parents tend to develop fixed patterns in which one is usually overadequate and the other inadequate. The overadequate-inadequate reciprocity and the decision paralysis create a state of extreme *functional helplessness* in the family.

There is an intense interdependence between father, mother and patient which we have called the "interdependent triad." It is usual for normal siblings to become rather involved in the family problem, but not so deeply that they cannot separate themselves from the triad, leaving the father, mother and patient interlocked in the family oneness. There are constant patterns of functioning within the triad. Either parent can have a close relationship with the patient, provided the other parent permits it. The parents, separated from each other by the emotional divorce, share the patient much as divorced parents share their children. The most familiar pattern is one in which the mother, in an extreme overadequate position to the helpless patient, has the "custody" of the patient, while the father is distant and passive. There are situations in which the mother-patient relationship is disrupted, following which the father then functions very much as does the mother in the close attachment to the patient.

The parents hold strong opposing viewpoints about many levels of issues in their lives together. The one issue about which there is strongest disagreement is the management of the patient. A father and mother with a high level of overt disagreement said, "We agree on everything but politics. Isn't that strange?" Other parents with a low level of overt disagreement said, "We agree on everything except how to raise children, and how to raise parakeets." It is important for the psychotherapist to know that the parents hold these opposite viewpoints about the patient, even though the opposing viewpoint is not expressed. Opposing viewpoints appear to be related more to opposing the other than to real strength of conviction. There have been exchanges of viewpoints in which each parent comes to argue the viewpoint formerly used by the other. The opposing viewpoints seem to function in the service of maintaining identity. For instance, the ones who "give in" have described a "loss of identity," "loss of part of myself," and "inability to know what I think and believe." "Speaking up" seems to be a way of maintaining identity. The "differences" constitute a pressing daily problem for the parents. To them, the answer lies in reaching an agreement and "that is impossible." Actually, their own effort to talk out the difference results in greater difference! The more clearly one states a viewpoint, the more vigorously the other raises the opposition.

Some definite *principles*, *rules* and *techniques* of family psychotherapy have been developed. The principles are derived directly from the working hypothesis. The rules establish the structure for adapting principles to the psychotherapy operation. The techniques are devices used by the therapist to implement the rules. For instance, one of the principles considers the family as a psychological unit. The rule requires the family to participate as a unit in the family psychotherapy. The techniques are devices used by the therapist to implement the rules. In this paper I shall focus on the more simple structure of a single family in family psychotherapy with one therapist, and avoid the more complex situations with multiple therapists and typical family groups.

The initial goal is to get the family unit into a continuing relationship with the therapist in which family members attempt to "work together" in the hour to discuss and define their own problems. The therapist works toward a position of unbiased detachment, from which position he is able to analyze intrafamily forces. If we think of the family as a single organism, the situation has certain analogies to the structure of psychoanalysis. The family "working together" is similar to the patient who attempts to free associate. The therapeutic effort is to analyze intrafamily relationships in situ, rather than to analyze the transference relationship between patient and analyst. When the therapist is successful in relating to the family unit and in avoiding individual relationships, the family unit develops a dependence on the therapist similar to neurotic transference, which is quite unlike the intense primitive attachment of psychotic patient to therapist.

We begin the psychotherapy with a simple explanation of the theoretical premise of the project and of the "working together" structure in the hours. The working together may appear simple on the surface but it is directed at the heart of the problem. The "emotional divorce," the "overadequate-inadequate reciprocity" and the problems of the "interdependent triad" stand in the way. The structure demands that one member function as leader and start the hour. When the family is able to start, deep anxiety is stirred up. There are definite mechanisms (equivalent to resistance in individual psychotherapy) by which the family avoids the anxiety of working together. When anxiety mounts, the family effort can become blocked. As I see it as this point, one of my main functions is that of an "enabler" who helps them get started at working together, who follows along when they can work together, and who helps them start again when there is a block.

A family with a psychotic family member is a functionally helpless organism, without a leader, and with a high level of overt anxiety. It has dealt helplessly and non-effectively with life, it has become dependent on outside experts for advice and guidance, and its most positive decisions are made in the service of relieving the anxiety of the moment, no matter how many complications this may cause tomorrow. How does the therapist help this kind of family into a working-together relationship? Some of our most important principles and rules are directed at this area. In broad terms, the goal is to find a leader in the leaderless family, to respect the family leader when there is a functioning leader, and to find ways to avoid individual relationships and the position of omnipotence into which the family attempts to place the therapist. A review of the research families will illustrate some of the problems with family leaders.

In the 15 families with fathers, there were 8 in which the mothers functioned clearly as the overadequate ones in relation to helpless patients and as decision-makers for the family. The fathers were distant, passive, resisting critics of the mothers' activities. Even though the fathers did not express it openly, their thoughts focused on what the mothers were doing wrong and on what the mothers should do to correct it, but not on any initiative or action for themselves. These mothers could motivate the family effort, overcome the fathers' and patients' resistance to coming to the hours and initiate the "working together." These families have done best in family psychotherapy.

There were four families in which the fathers functioned as spokesmen for the mothers, who remained behind the scenes. A parody of this situation might go as follows: The mother tells the father that he has to decide what to do. He says he doesn't know what to do. She tells him he has to decide and then gives him an idea to help him decide. He says he will do it that way. Such a father is as helpless as he was when his own mother told him what to do, what to wear or when to get a haircut. With this family in the unstructured working-together situation, the helplessness of the father is clearly demonstrated. He has to begin the hour. He turns to the mother. In this situation she is silent, although she may lecture him after the hour ends. Then he turns to the therapist, using all his ingenious mechanisms to have the therapist tell him what to do. These families have done poorest in family psychotherapy. One family went over a year before the parents could begin to work together. The fathers are skillful at reading "instructions" into the therapist's facial expressions or casual remarks.

There were three families in which the fathers appeared to have functioned as the leaders and decision-makers, but they were comparatively weak and more like "acting leaders." The mothers were active with the patients, but in relation to the fathers they were relatively silent. They seemed to be important somewhere behind the scenes. One of these mothers finally explained her version of this. She said, "If I make a direct suggestion, he opposes it. So, I keep working it around and eventually it will come out of him as his idea. The only problem is that he often misses the point and changes it around, and then I have to start all over." These families made slow progress in family psychotherapy.

It was relatively easy for the overadequate decision-making mothers to initiate working together. Two mothers were able to start at the beginning of the first hour. The mother, separated from the father by the emotional divorce, would direct the first comment to the patient. If anxiety was high she would criticize the patient. If anxiety was low, she might use an understanding approach, such as, "Tell us what you think. Tell us what you don't like about us." Eventually there would be an angry exchange between mother and patient. The passive father, in silent disagreement with the mother, would remain quiet, expecting the therapist to "put her right." Later he might ask the therapist to express a professional opinion. The request for a professional opinion usually comes when there is a difference of opinion between the parents. The therapist who expresses an opinion not only takes a side, but also misses the "why" of the question. In the disharmony between mother and patient, the father usually identifies with the patient's viewpoint, yet, when the patient asks him for support, he remains passive. If the patient becomes aggressive with the mother, he will respond to the mother's request to make the patient behave. The decision-making mother can become very aggressive and even cruel in her attempts to deal with the family.

In the beginning we tended to point out the mother's aggression, the illogic of her comments, and the father's passivity. This would result in the mother's stopping the aggression and, along with it, giving up the position of family leader. The therapist could then find himself faced with a helpless "what do we do now" family. The passive father would usually respond with a half-hearted attempt to be more active, but with a compliant "the doctor told me to" attitude. Now we avoid comments which might reduce the initiative of the family leader. We make comments designed to "support" the family leader, such as, "You are having a hard time trying to get your family to pull together." These people have lived together for years. They are all perfectly capable of dealing with each other, even though they themselves might fear that they are harmful to each other. When the therapist is able to deal with his own concerns, then the family members are more capable of utilizing their own spontaneous resources. Eventually the passive father moves, on his own initiative, to oppose the aggressive mother, and the main conflict shifts from the mother-patient relationship to the mother-father relationship. The father usually retreats when the mother becomes angry, anxious or tearful but eventually he can maintain a stand that is "no longer soluble in the mother's tears." It is an important milestone when the father can maintain his strong position. The mother will go through a few days of intense anxiety and then settle down to a period of calm, kind, firm objectivity. One such mother said, "I am so pleased with him. If he can keep on being a man, I can be a woman." This new level will continue a few days or a few weeks before they lapse back to the familiar dominant mother-passive father positions, but after the first such shift, it is easier for new shifts to occur.

My opinion about the "dominating" mother has been changed by this experience. As long as she feels the weight of the family problem, she is highly motivated for change. If the therapist can keep her in that position, she can cause the family to change. However, she will relax her effort and turn the problem over to the therapist at the first opportunity. For instance, she will ask the therapist to convince the father to give up his opposition to the family psychotherapy. She is quite capable of dealing with the father but the therapist will fail. If the therapist tries to help her deal with the family, he will suddenly discover that she has changed to a helpless complaining person who waits for him to motivate her helpless family. Some of the most significant family changes have occurred when the mothers have become "fed up" and have exploded in anger. One mother said, "I wish I could get mad more often. Acting mad doesn't work. I have to be really mad." Most of our therapeutic impasses have occurred when we have failed to identify the family leader. The therapist tells the family he expects one member to be the responsible spokesman for the family on arrangement concerning the psychotherapy. The family can change the spokesman as it wishes, as long as the therapist has one person who can speak for the family. The selection of spokesman forces the family to a beginning resolution of the leadership problem. It also creates a workable structure for the therapist.

There are a number of mechanisms to avoid the anxiety of working together. The most prominent is the effort to involve the therapist in individual relationships. This mechanism, and techniques for dealing with it, are discussed throughout the paper. There are frequent joking comments about the working together, such as, "We do that at home. How can that help?" One father who had previously been in individual psychotherapy said, "Doesn't it strike you as crazy for us to come here to say the same things we could say at home?" The therapist responded, "Any crazier than for you to go to a therapist alone and act as though he were your father?" A subtle and difficult mechanism is one by which the parents represent the psychotic one as the therapist's patient and themselves as assistant therapists. The assistants become helpless and the therapist is responsible for three helpless individuals. The parents may urge the patient to talk and thus create a situation in which the patient fills the time with psychotic chatter while the parents attempt to enlist the therapist in interpreting symbolic meaning. Several of the families, from their long experience with psychiatry, had an excellent intellectual grasp of psychoanalytic theory. Another mechanism is "chit-chat." Silence can occur in less disturbed families. When the family is disturbed, the one with the highest anxiety will start chattering. The more functionally helpless the family, the more ingenious the family at invoking these mechanisms. The families with fathers who spoke for the mother were the most skillful in the use of avoidance mechanisms.

The avoidance mechanisms that involve the therapist in the emotional problems of the individual are of more immediate importance to the family psychotherapy than the avoidance mechanisms that are contained within the family unit. The family is not able to work together successfully, nor is the therapist able to see the family unit objectively when he is emotionally involved with a single family member. It probably is not possible for the therapist to relate to the family without occasional involvements with individuals. My efforts have gone toward recognizing individual involvements when they occur, and toward finding more efficient ways to regain and to maintain emotional detachment. An important part of the therapist's over involvement comes from his own unconscious functioning. For instance, when I feel myself inwardly cheering the hero, or hating the villain in the family drama, or pulling for the family victim to assert himself, I consider it time for me to work on my own functioning. Some of our most important psychotherapy rules have been made to structure an environment favorable for the therapy. Note taking has been an efficient device to help me remain detached. The rationale for the detachment and for my use of note taking to achieve this is explained to the family at the beginning of treatment.

Family members are skillful at making individual communications outside the family psychotherapy hours. They will stop at the end of the hour to tell the therapist something "too unimportant for the family hour." They write personal notes, make telephone calls between hours, or find occasion to tell the therapist "secrets" about other family members that the therapist should know, but that would be "hurtful" if mentioned in the family hour. Not all of these communications are "loaded," but a blanket rule that the therapist will report all outside communications at the next family hour was successful in preventing emotional involvements that resulted from certain of these individual messages.

There are times when, for reality reasons such as illness or business, it is not possible for a family member to attend hours. In the beginning we had a strict rule that a family hour would not be possible unless at least two family members were present. This rule was designed to prevent an individual relationship with a single family member. Recently we have been making one exception to the two-person rule. When the family leader is not motivated to overcome family resistance we see the leader alone, but the orientation remains on the family, the leader is seen as the official representative of the family, and discussion of the leader's personal problems is avoided. For instance, one family leader began the hour by talking about her own fears. The therapist shifted the discussion to the family problem. Personal material will eventually emerge in the family sessions when it is possible to see the emotional reaction of other family members to the personal material. Results from seeing the leader alone have been good. When the other parent is alone, he will represent himself as sick or helpless, or solicit aid in dealing with the leader's injustice. When the patient is seen alone, the parents relax their efforts and leave the problem between patient and therapist.

The therapist remains relatively inactive when the family is able to work together. We have continued as long as 12 consecutive hours with no more comment than a greeting at the beginning of the hour and an announcement that time was up. In one such period, the father asked what the therapist was supposed to do in the hours. The therapist replied, "I create the atmosphere. It is my presence that counts." The father began calling the therapist "Dr. Presence." When the working together goes smoothly, communication barriers begin to decrease. Those in the controlled, inhibited families find it is possible to express thoughts in the family hours that could not be expressed at home. One mother said, "It is a revelation to come here and find out so many things about the others that I never knew before." Those in the fighting, arguing families find they can talk much more calmly than at home. One father said, "We have stopped fighting at home. We agreed to reserve the emotional issues and the fights until we get here. We do not get as mad here and it is harder to get mad and walk out." The period of free communication will stop when the communications again arouse anxiety. Then there is a period of resistance with comments such as, "We are getting nowhere. The family situation is worse than when we started." From experience, we have found that certain "feeling" communications arouse deep anxiety, which can be followed by emotional arguments over trivial points. It can be fairly easy for the family to resume working together if the therapist can relate the "explosion" to the specific feeling communication.

There are inquiries about the kinds of comments and interpretations we make in family psychotherapy. There is infinite material of interest to any psychotherapist. The working together, the family leader structure, and the emotional detachment of the therapist always get immediate attention. Comments about intrafamily avoidance mechanisms are withheld until the therapist can speak without impeding the working together. A comment that causes the family to shift attention from its own problems to the therapist was probably ill-timed. The family member in the most helpless position (usually the patient) tells dramatic stories of trauma, rejection, hardship and injustice. Other family members disagree with the reality of the stories. If the therapist becomes involved in the dramatic stories, he can lose his way in a swamp of conflicting detail. We avoid content interpretations and focus on the process. Detailed content material for the research was obtained in separate information-gathering meetings. Such comments as, "The mother uses one voice in speaking to the patient, and another voice in speaking to the father" and "The father looks at the patient when he speaks to him, but not at the mother when he speaks to her," seem to be helpful at any time. The more therapists have limited their comments, the more active family members become in interpreting for each other. For a time we followed the practice of "summing up" at the end of the hour. Families began to stop five minutes before the end to wait on "the word" from the therapist. When family members were asked to do their own summaries, they were able to do rather well.

One of our most important principles has to do with the therapist's attitude about anxiety. These families have a low tolerance for anxiety. They fear it, withdraw from it, and treat it as an awful thing to be avoided at any cost. They compromise important life principles for "peace at any price." The anxiety inhibits every relationship in the family. The parents are afraid to relate spontaneously with each other lest they do or say something to "hurt" the other. Parents are particularly afraid to relate to the patient. Convinced they did something "wrong" to cause the problem in the patient, they are afraid to touch the patient lest they make the problem worse. In family psychotherapy, the families quickly encounter deep anxiety. It is essential that the therapist have some way to help them with the anxiety. Throughout the entire course of family psychotherapy, the therapist maintains an attitude which conveys, "Anxiety is inevitable if you solve the problem. When anxiety increases, one has to decide whether to give in and retreat or carry on in spite of it. Anxiety does not harm people. It only makes them uncomfortable. It can cause you to shake, or lose sleep, or become confused, or develop physical symptoms, but it will not kill you and it will subside. People can even grow and become more mature by having to face and deal with anxiety situations. Do you have to go on treating each other as fragile people who are about to fall apart?"

In my opinion these families are not really helpless. They are functionally helpless. The parents are adequate, resourceful people in their outside relationships. It is in relationship to each other that they become functionally helpless. When the family is able to be a contained unit, and there is a family leader with motivation to define the problem and to back his own convictions in taking appropriate action, the family can change from a directionless, anxiety-ridden, floundering unit, to a more resourceful organism with a problem to be solved. The parents had all spent years seeking answers outside themselves. They had read extensively, attended lectures, and sought the advice of experts for answers to what they had done "wrong" and what they should do "right." When parents could eventually reach the point of acting on convictions from inside themselves, they might do things that others would consider harmful, but the patient and the rest of the family would respond positively.

In the effort to focus on the family, the parents' emphasis on the "sickness" of the patient was defocused. For example, a son who avoided stepping on cracks in the sidewalk was upset unless the father also avoided the cracks. The father, to avoid hurting the son, went along with this irrational behavior.[3] The father focused on changing the "sickness" in the son. The therapist asked how the father managed to get himself into the position of skipping over cracks. At the beginning of treatment all the parents were solicitous and infantilizing to the sick, incompetent patients. As the parents began to assume leadership responsibility, there would be arguments between the parents about the patient. One parent, basing opinion on "knowing how the patient felt," would say that behavior was caused by "sickness" and advocate understanding, love and kindness for the patient. The other parent would conclude that it was not all "sickness" and advocate management based on what the patient did, instead of feelings. The arguments seemed to have little to do with the functioning of the patient at the time. In those families in which both parents could eventually tone down the sickness theme and relate to the patient on a reality level, the patients changed. After one family had emerged from their unreality, the patient said, "As long as they called me sick and treated me sick, I somehow had to act sick. When they stopped treating me sick, I had a choice of acting sick or acting well."

Individuals in the family went through a process of "differentiation of self" from other family members. An important part was emotional differentiation. One mother said she was putting an invisible wall between herself and the daughter, "so I can feel what I feel and she can feel what she feels; so I can have my life and she can have hers." It was common for the mother's tears to "hurt" the rest of the family more than the mother. The therapist asked many questions to define the emotional overlap between family members. Another part of the differentiation was the "establishment of identity" which is similar to the discovery of self in individual psychotherapy. An example was a father who said, "If we spent less time working on our son and more time trying to find out what we believe and what we stand for, it would be easier for him to find himself." The family leaders were the first to begin working on differentiation of self. The other parent changed more slowly, usually in relation to the leader parent. When the family leader changed, the new leader was the one who changed next. The patients usually lagged far behind; their changes came after the parents were fairly definite about themselves.

There was one family which illustrates the degree to which parents go along with irrational behavior, the dramatic change when a passive father took a positive stand, and the marked change when the therapist refused to call the patient "sick."

The 17-year-old psychotic son was the only child of parents in their early forties. He dominated the home with his psychosis. A guidance center recommended hospitalization. The parents wanted to keep the son at home. They were referred to our family project for a consultation. There was no space on the "in-residence" ward, but we agreed to outpatient family psychotherapy as long as the parents would maintain the son at home.

The son spent much time in his room with the door locked. He insisted that window blinds be closed to prevent attack from enemies outside. He crawled across the floor beneath the windows lest his enemies see through the blinds. He became angry unless his mother sat with feet and hands in a certain position. He would demand special food, throw it in the garbage because the mother did not prepare it right, and demand more.

The first hour the therapist did little more than wonder how the parents came to be privates and the son the general in the family. The father made a weak effort to take a stand. The son twisted the father's arm. A dramatic change came after 4 months (18 hours) of family psychotherapy. The son had been unusually aggressive and the parents unusually helpless. The father expressed concern that the son might kill him. The therapist suggested hospitalization if this was the case. The father said he would not attend.

The next hour he was going on vacation and would let the mother and patient settle their own differences. Father, mother and son were together for the next hour, three days later. The family was calm and congenial; there were no psychotic symptoms. After the previous hour the father had announced that he was tired living in a darkened morgue and that he was going to open the blinds to let the sunshine in. The son threatened to kill the father if he touched the blinds. The father opened the blinds. The father and son fought briefly and the father won. The psychotic symptoms disappeared. The father policed the home for a month. The son did well. The father-son relationship had changed and the son-mother relationship had changed, but the father-mother relationship did not change.

After a month the father told the mother he could not take it any longer. He gave up his firm stand, the mother resumed her picking on the son, and the son resumed the psychosis. The family continued some months with the chronic psychotic adjustment. There was a pattern in which the parents would "gang up" on the son to prove him "sick" and the son would argue vigorously, using paranoid delusions to support his arguments. The parents would then use the delusions as proof of sickness. In an effort to give more status to the son, the therapist referred to the family as a debating society, indicating that debating rules permit the debater to argue illogical points if he wishes. The son kept arguing, but within a week he was choosing to argue reality points to support his viewpoints. After 16 months (73 family psychotherapy hours) the son said, "For years I have been trying to find what to do about my parents' brainwashing me. Now I know. The trick is to brainwash them before they brainwash me."

The family achieved a good symptomatic result. They reduced appointments to once a month and continued for 94 hours over 3 years. The son made a good social adjustment. He finished high school and went on to college. The mother is employed for the first time in her life.

This was a family with an "acting leader" father. The parents in these families have not achieved as much basic change in the parental relationship as families with more definite family leaders.

Outside the formal research study we have used family psychotherapy in a number of families with character disorders and neurotic problems. The family relationship patterns first observed in the "in residence" families were also presenting all other families. However, there were also striking difference. In families with neurotic problems, the patterns were more flexible and resilient. The separation in the emotional divorce could be as great but it could fluctuate more easily. The "overadequate-inadequate reciprocity" could be as marked but there was not so much anxiety, rigidity and decision paralysis. In families with severe character disorders, the family relationship patterns appeared to be essentially the same as in families with psychoses. Families with neuroses were much better able to distinguish feeling from fact and to act on the basis of reality. Families with psychotic-level problems were more inclined to evaluate a situation with feelings, to consider the feelings as factual, and to act on the basis of feeling. Families with neurotic problems were more capable of objective consideration of the problem without "acting it out," involving the therapist, and becoming paralyzed by indecision. According to my current thinking, there is nothing in schizophrenia that is not also present in all of us. Schizophrenia is made up of the essence of human experience many times distilled. With our incapacity to look at ourselves, we have much to learn about ourselves from studying the least mature of us.

In considering change in the research families, we have come to think more in terms of change in the parental relationship than of change in psychotic symptoms. The parents can change in relationship to each other. When there is a change in the fixed rigidity of the parental relationship, there follows a change in the patient, irrespective of the immediate level of psychotic symptoms. Psychotic symptoms can change dramatically in relation to one parent. There have been other examples of temporary change similar to the change in the family described above. The most characteristic and definite changes occurred in outpatient families with decision-making mothers. The most dramatic changes occurred when the fathers assumed family leadership against the mother's protests. This was usually followed by a period of calm resolution of the emotional divorce and objectivity in taking stands against the patients' demands. Then the patients would change. Until observing these shifts, we had considered "dominant mothers" and "passive fathers" as fixed personality characteristics. The fathers would lapse into inactivity, passively permit the mothers to resume the leadership, and a new cycle would begin. These shifts were repeated once or twice a year, with successive shifts becoming calmer and easier.

One family went on to a fairly good resolution of parental relationship problems. The patient achieved a good adjustment. Two other families, still in family psychotherapy, appear to be going in this direction. Two families terminated psychotherapy in helpless disharmony when the family-leader structure was lost. Two families with "acting leader" fathers, including the family described in this paper, achieved gradual symptomatic improvement with minimal change in the parental relationship. The outpatient families did much better in family psychotherapy. This did not appear directly related to the long-term maximum degree of psychosis in most of the in-residence patients. The degree of chronic impairment was almost as great in some of the outpatient families. The seven in-residence father families, with hospital staff nearby, were never able to deal with their helplessness. One in-residence family achieved some change between the parents and, with two other families, sufficient decrease in symptoms for the patients to live at home. Four families participated only six months. In two of these there was no change. The patients are in institutions. The other two families are now in outpatient family psychotherapy.

SUMMARY

This paper describes a method of family psychotherapy developed as part of a family research project. The research was based on the theoretical premise "the family as the unit of illness." The psychotherapeutic approach "the family as the unit of treatment" was developed from the theoretical premise and incorporated as an integral part of the research project. The goal of this paper has been to present a broad over-all view of both the theoretical and clinical aspects of the psychotherapy. To achieve this, the theoretical premise "the family as the unit of illness" has been described in some detail. The description of family psychotherapy has been focused more on broad principles and the rationale for structuring the psychotherapy than on description and clinical details.

REFERENCES

1. Bowen, Murray, *Family Participation in Schizophrenia*, Presented at annual meeting, American Psychiatric Assoc., Chicago, May 1957.
2. Bowen, M., R. H. Dysinger, W. M. Brodey, and B. Basamania, *Study and Treatment of Five Hospitalized Families Each with a Psychotic Member.* Presented at annual meeting, American Orthopsychiatric Assoc., Chicago, March 1957.
3. Bowen, Murray. "A Family Concept of Schizophrenia," in *The Etiology of Schizophrenia* (D. Jackson, Ed.). New York: Basic Books, 1960.
4. Richardson, H. B. *Patients Have Families.* New York: Commonwealth Fund, 1948.
5. Bowen, M., R. H. Dysinger, and B. Basamania. *The Role of the Father in Families with a Schizophrenic Patient,* Am. J. Psychiatry, 115:117–120, 1959.
6. Bowen, Murray. "Family Relationships in Schizophrenia," in *Schizophrenia-An Integrated Approach* (Alfred Auerback, Ed.). New York: Ronald Press, 1959.
7. Lidz T., and S. Fleck. "Schizophrenia, Human Integration and the Role of the Family," in *The Etiology of Schizophrenia* (D. Jackson, Ed.) New York Basic Books, 1960.

NOTES

1. Total families for the entire project. The numbers reported in individual papers are different, depending on the number with whom each author had individual experience.
2. The detailed hypothesis has been presented in other papers (1, 2, 3).
3. Lidz and Fleck (7) have referred to this as the families who provide training in irrationality.

The Family as the Unit of Study and Treatment
Workshop, 1959
2. A Family Perspective on the Diagnosis of
Individual Members
Robert H. Dysinger, M.D.
*Psychiatrist, Adult Psychiatry Branch, Clinical Investigations,
National Institute of Mental Health, Bethesda, Maryland*

The French poet Paul Valery in a dialogue titled "Socrates and His Physician"[1] wrote as follows. (Socrates is ill and speaks to his Physician Eryximachus, who has said he will be well the next day.)

Socrates: If you show me you know me better than I do myself, Whilst I find myself at present quite overwhelmed and full of disgust, must I not conclude that my whole effort is puerile that my intimate tactics vanish in the face of your entirely exterior art, which envelopes thereby capturing as a single stroke the universe of my person?

Eryximachus: Do not make me so formidable, great Socrates—I am not the master of knowledge and power which you create you yourself! My limitations are all too certain.

I for my part am concerned only with phenomena, inside the complexity and confusion of which I try to find my bearings, so as to bring as much solace as possible to the humans who consult me; and, in the course of doing so, to cause them the least ill (for the physician must fear his art and not make an unreserved use of its weapons).

It is true I know you better than you do yourself . . . in so far as you are ignorant of yourself, but infinitely less well in so far as you know yourself.

Diagnosis may be recognized as a specific function of the clinician in using his professional skill to attempt to identify the presence of a health problem and to define its nature. The clinician's diagnostic functioning operates in relation to a parallel areas of functioning in the person who consults him. Before consulting a clinician the person has concerned himself with a problem in his own experience, estimated its relevance to his health, considered gauged whether it was getting better or worse, decided whether to give it serious attention or not, and if so, how to proceed. When the result is a decision to consult a particular clinician, the person presents a derivative of his "diagnosis" functioning which the clinician makes note of, often in his patient's words, as the presenting problem. It becomes the starting point in working toward his clinical diagnosis.

These statements are presented to focus attention on the fact that for any individual there exists a describable area of continuous psychological functioning that has to do with his views and action concerning his own health.

In this paper an attempt is made to consider this area of functioning independent of whether a significant health problem exists. The focus is on questions of the following sort: How accurate are the person's observations of his own experience? How well does he distinguish between things relevant to health and those less relevant? How does he distinguish between how he feels about his health and how he estimates whether or not there is a significant problem? To what extent does he attempt to come to terms with such questions? To what extent does he leave this to others? In functioning in this area are there characteristic ways in which he is inaccurate and ineffective? Is he aware of them and does he take them into account? How well does he deal with the clinician in the interests of his own health?

In functioning about health matters a person operates in many relationships other than the clinical one. The standard social inquiries and comments about how well or ill people look are an indication that health matters are at least touched on in most relationships. It would appear that there is a special involvement in family relationships about health matters. The adequacy of the functioning about health matters of individuals and families is obviously relevant to health.

A project which undertook intensive psychotherapy and clinical study of family groups who lived in a special ward setting afforded an unusually rich and detailed view of family functioning. This paper is devoted to a discussion of some of the characteristic functioning about health matters of intensively studied family groups, consisting of both parents and a schizophrenic son or daughter. In the discussion the family members are referred to as mother, father, child and sibling. The terms child, son and daughter refer to the schizophrenic member and not to the siblings.

The striking general pattern that became apparent in the study of the series of families is that the mother, father, and son or daughter participate in an intense emotional process with one another in which health issues are consistently involved. For each, dealing about a health matter independent of the intense emotion appears to be conditional on first attaining a psychological distance that amounts to going out of contact with at least one of the other two. This chronic pattern was not seen in the relationships with the siblings except infrequently and for short periods. In the mother-father-child group a poor night's sleep, poor appetite, a missed meal, an experience of anxiety, a mild failure, a change in weight, an upper respiratory infection, easily becomes the focus of emotional views that see them as matters with serious health implications. Actions based on these views often follow which regularly further complicate the situation. It is difficult for any of the three to achieve a view of health difficulties of his own or of the other two that is objective enough to be workable. It is difficult for him to be aware that his view may be largely a feeling, and that the belief in its accuracy is related more to the intensity of the feeling than to consistency with the facts.

The distinction between feelings and fact is blurred. A sick feeling is often dealt with as though it is evidence in itself that a definite illness is present. Strange feelings are often handled as though their presence is in itself evidence of serious mental disorder. Anxiety is regularly regarded as evidence of some kind of disease. This trend was highlighted by the contrasting observation that when normal siblings were anxious or felt bad the same parents could take a calm view, and be fairly realistic in estimating the situation and proceed to do what they could to help with it. The inaccuracies in estimating matters in the health area are often entertained with little recognition of the possibility that they might be in error and out of proportion. The nice distinction between a somatized feeling and a physical symptom is difficult for family members to grasp, in spite of a good deal of experience with both. The family functioning was much more realistic and adequate in the few experiences with major acute physical illness that occurred during the period of study.

When it comes to doing something effective about a health matter, the families are in serious difficulty. They regularly decide and do things for each other in this area. Each of them sees the problem differently so that real accord between any two is rare. In the service of getting things done one of the three is often deferred to. Many things become stalemated and put off or solved with an inadequate compromise.

The mother regularly functions in the position of family diagnostician. She is the one who decides when someone is sick, what is the matter, and what should be done about it, not only for herself, but also for her husband and children. She is poorly equipped to do this job effectively especially when she is anxious. She is inaccurate, hasty, full of urgency and over sure of herself, and often gives her feelings about such things the weight of certain knowledge and can entertain only with great difficulty the idea that she may have missed the point completely. She often sees a problem in herself as a problem in the patient or the husband. When she is fairly accurate she has difficulty in dealing with it except as an emergency. She is inclined to quickly give the problem a name, often a medical term, speak urgently and seriously about it and proceed to do things that would confirm it and get something done. Considerations of practical workability are often missed.

She has considerable capacity to get others to see things her way and to see those who would differ as obviously wrong. The patient member is of course the one with whom this process is most intense and continuous, and is the one who uses the most extreme measures to deal with it. These include a passive going along and being what is diagnosed, thus becoming a living confirmation of what is often an inaccurate diagnosis, being impossible in a way that sabotages the view of the other, a passive resistance, open defiance, or ignoring.

The father who participates in the arrangement gives the mother the position of the family diagnostician and appears to accept her judgment as better than his own. He often gives a greater weight to her estimates and recommendations about his own problems when his opinion makes more sense. One father said in all seriousness, "My wife knows more about my stomach than I do." At times situations have occurred that would support the idea that he has indirectly asked his wife to do this for him and the wife has reluctantly agreed; at other times in the same family it would appear that the wife has actively taken over this position and the husband has let her have it in order to avoid an open fight about it.

The mother, father, and sibling are usually able to reach a workable decision about a health matter. But this is achieved with the son or daughter only after great labor if at all. The mother's point of view regularly prevails on important issues, the father either remaining distant and ignoring, or passively going along with it. At times he becomes his wife's agent in carrying out her plan. He may have difficulty in making it work, and then she may offer suggestions or complain about how he goes about it. He can then resign as her agent and leave the matter up to her. After a complaint about uncooperativeness she might try and fail. The mother may then turn the problem over to the father who may then have a chance to deal with it his way. He then may try to fail, sometimes from subtle sabotage by the mother.

In passing, it is worth mentioning that an awareness of this repeating process has been helpful, since the clinician may easily find himself in a position like that of the father without knowing it. It is an impression that this is commonly set in motion when he tacitly agrees with the mother's view that an anxious situation is a medical emergency, and tries to deal with it for her.

The intense involvement about health matters in the mother-father-child group is most openly active with respect to the child. He is consistently dealt with by the parents as though he were seriously ill, quite fragile, and in danger of losing what health he has if a great effort is not made. There has been a consistent paradoxical phenomenon that this view is expressed most emphatically just after he has made a clear gain. In the course of one discussion, a son made a telling point to his father when he said, "Just because you don't agree with me, you don't have to call me sick." It would appear that an actual improvement in the patient unsettles the emotional equilibrium of the family to increase the parents' anxiety that manifests itself in turn by an increase in gratuitous diagnostic activity with the consequence at times of a loss of the gain. A similar pattern is seen between the parents.

The functioning about health matters was highlighted in the use of medical service by individual family members. One striking observation about the mothers was the emotional pressure on the physician for agreement with the mother's own specific diagnosis and an obtuseness in making use of his clinical judgment. Most of the mothers were anxiously devoted to home remedies, diets, vitamins, and some specific medication or other health routine. Several had believed for years that they had one or more physical illnesses of which there was no clinical evidence.

The fathers made less active use of medical services and characteristically presented themselves apologetically, as though there was little clarity about the problem. They often spoke of what the wife thinks, what a previous physician said, and had difficulty in getting to the point. Where the mothers tended to see a routine problem as a serious emergency, the fathers tended to pass off a significant problem as probably trivial. The mother was often active in getting in on her husband's medical dealings with the doctor.

When the daughter or son was able to arrange his own appointment he was often more to the point and the matter was easier to settle than was the case with either parent. The main difficulty appeared to be considerable apprehensiveness about seeing the physician and difficulty in getting to him without being either brought or sent by the parents.

In summary, the functioning of a series of families about health matters is characterized by an intense emotional process in which the mother, father and child are deeply involved with one another. Thinking about health questions is heavily in the service of feelings, with marked impairment of objectivity and of effective action. The impairment is apparent whether the difficulty is a physical or an emotional one; the distinction between the two is regularly blurred, and one mistaken for the other. There is often little awareness that judgment in this area is undependable. The emotional process easily involves others, especially the clinician, and can make it most difficult for him to function responsibly. The past histories indicate that this situation has existed for many years.

A description of one series of events in the clinical course of one family is presented for illustration. These episodes were selected from many since they seemed to be related and to represent the unfolding of a single theme over a few months' time.

The father was in his early sixties, the mother in her early fifties, a schizophrenic son in his twenties, and there were three younger siblings. The son had lived at home in a chronic placid withdrawn state for several years following a year's hospitalization for an acute schizophrenic psychosis. There was serious financial difficulty as a consequence of a gradual decline of the father's income over several years' time. The family as a group gave an initial general impression of a tired, over controlled group of people with little spontaneity.

The issue to be described made its first appearance in a psychotherapy meeting as an open emotional argument between the father and the son, who shared the same room. The father was objecting to the son's insistence that the amount of artificial light in the room was too great for him. He was emphasizing that he needed light to do his work. The mother, as was characteristic for her in such arguments, took the position of the mediating peacemaker who urges more understanding, this time tipping her comments slightly in favor of the son's comfort. To this the father made no comment. An uneasy peace followed with the father favoring the son by observing a lights-off policy after 9 p.m. and finding another place to work after that hour.

After a period in which the father was making a diligent effort to avoid stepping on his son's sensitive points, and tiptoeing about to avoid an issue, he seemed to tire of this and with considerable anxiety undertook to do something about it by arranging to move his son to another room. To his surprise and pleasure, the son presented no opposition and proceeded to help with the moving.

Shortly after this another meeting occurred in which the mother was speaking of the value of a well-illuminated cheerful décor and bright cheery attitudes in improving the household atmosphere. The son was mild in taking a differing view that artificial illumination was not to his liking; in fact he was opposed to it in principle. The mother developed the opinion that if the light bothered him as much as it seemed to, this confirmed her idea that something was definitely wrong with his eyes and he should see the doctor about it. The son cautiously expressed the view that he didn't see the problem that way. The father entered the discussion at this point, adding reasons to those of the mother about why this would be a good idea. This prompted the son to a more vigorous expression of his view to the father, to the effect that although the light did bother his eyes, he didn't see it now as something to see a doctor about, but if he ever thought that advisable he would take care of it. His discussion shifted to a more conversational one between the parents on the same subject, in which the father with a quiet chuckle ventured a comment about his lifelong enjoyment of firesides and of retiring and rising with the sun. The mother did not respond.

Some time later the mother consulted the physician about "eyestrain" she had been having for some time, more marked of late, especially noticeable in connection with reading. She thought it was due to a worsening with age of a refractive error diagnosed by an optometrist friend two years before. She had worn bifocals for reading since that time. She represented the optical problem as being serious enough to absolutely require glasses for reading, but further discussion revealed that she at times read at length without the glasses and without difficulty. Although the difficulty was presented as though it were serious and perhaps ominous, her concern about the matter was far greater than the difficulty associated with it and she recognized this. The detailed history of the occasions of distress appeared to follow a pattern different than would be expected with a simple optical problem. When the physician responded by saying that he thought there was a very good chance that her estimate of this problem was quite possible that there was no major optical problem, she responded by saying, "Do you really think so?" as though pleasantly surprised. The doctor added that it was his impression that there was a good possibility that the distress was an anxiety manifestation and that a careful eye examination would help clarify the matter. The mother then spoke for the first time of a longstanding problem with her son about glasses. He has worn glasses consistently until the acute psychosis developed. At that time he smashed them and refused her offer to replace them. He had not worn them since, even though the family had supplied him with a new pair when he returned home. These he had promptly lost. She spoke of this as though reviewing out loud an old story that she seeing more clearly than she did before. The consultation ended with a discussion of arrangements for an eye examination. This was later done and revealed a "small" refractive error insufficient to account for the difficulty.

This series of events is seen as the unfolding, in a few months, of an issue in which the mother, father, and patient were all initially involved. It was first apparent as a conflict between the father and the son which the father acted to settle, then as a difference between the mother and son which the son's stand ended, and then as a somatic distress in the mother clarified in a discussion with the physician.

A medical experience with another mother was an important lesson in the subtlety with which the family problem can involve the clinical situation.

She had consulted the physician about whether her fingers showed any evidence of early arthritis. The matter was considered and apparently resolved satisfactorily around the point that there was no indication of arthritis. At a different time she requested that an order be written for vitamins since the family was in the habit of using them and it was some convenience to have them available in this way. After explicit statements to the effect that he saw no medical indication either for or against their use, the doctor agreed to write the order to accommodate the family. Some months later the medical policy was changed to one of writing orders for medication only when specifically indicated for diagnosed medical problems. When the significance of the policy change for the vitamin order was presented to the mother, she responded in all seriousness to the effect that she didn't understand why she couldn't have the vitamins for her arthritis any more. The doctor was amazed to learn that it was apparently her view of some months' standing that she had arthritis, that he also thought so, and that the vitamins were an indicated treatment for it. He had meanwhile been quite satisfied that he had, at some pains, been effective in presenting his opinion and that the matter was settled satisfactorily. It did not become clear until the policy change was implemented that this was definitely not the case, and that the doctor had been ordering vitamins which had been taken as his treatment for an arthritis that in his stated opinion did not exist.

There are further points about family functioning in the health area that may be noted by focusing on the way the series of families presented their situation initially and proceeded to arrange with the project for clinical service. Of ten families[2] which, after the initial discussions, proceeded to arrange for clinical service, the mother was the active spokesman in five and the father in the remaining five. In two of the families whose participation was arranged for by the mother, the father began as a reluctant participant. In those arranged for by the father, there were none in which the mother participated reluctantly. In other families which after the initial discussions did not proceed to arrange for clinical attention, there were several where the father was spokesman and definitely interested, and the mother was reluctant. The experience is consistent with the idea that a mother's reluctance has the effect of precluding the step toward arranging for clinical attention while the father's does not. The father is the active family spokesman in about half of the cases; the experience suggests that he can proceed effectively from this position only when the mother is also interested.

The presenting proposition is regularly that the family problem is the son or daughter, and that it is a matter of illness. The intensity and regularity of this presenting family view becomes a more impressive fact when seen in the context of further developments. It soon becomes apparent that other serious issues exist; such things as a possible divorce, long-neglected gross medical problems, serious financial difficulties, and chronic deadlock between the parents on major family decisions are also in the picture. There is room to wonder how it is that the psychosis becomes such a central issue.

This consideration gains further weight when it is observed that initially in the family therapy situation attention is for some time almost completely devoted to the schizophrenic member. When the parents attempt to deal with other things and encounter anxiety, the discussion regularly returns to the child. A major theme of the discussion is that the problem in the family is the incapacity of the son or daughter, who is seen as physically fragile and unable to understand things or do very much. At the same time there are many suggestions and advice about many things that the child might do that would make a difference. The inconsistency in this had gone unrecognized for some time.

The indications are that the process of arranging for clinical help and the manner of proceeding with it may be, in significant part, another evidence of the operation of emotional processes in the functioning about health matters.

If this is substantially correct, there would be an indication for the clinician to find a way to deal with his diagnostic function in such a way that he avoids lending the weight of clinical authority to the inaccuracies involved. The clinician's position in accomplishing this is delicate. He has a professional responsibility to name a diagnosis, and a current clinical fact to recognize in the form of an obviously impaired person. The family mechanism can operate to insist that he agree with the parental view. A different view, if presented effectively at all, would necessarily encounter anxiety. Even a response that is carefully limited to recognizing what is already obvious carries with it the implication that the impaired functioning of the child is the only problem worthy of clinical description. The use of the term "patient" to designate only this member of the family has a similar implication. It may well be that a satisfactory answer to the problem of diagnosis may be available when it is possible to achieve a view of the problem at a family level.

In conclusion, the observations described here may be used as a basis for venturing one kind of statement that would attempt to recognize the problem at a family level. Could it be that the situation is something like this? An intense emotional problem in the parental relationship has long been handled through a complicated and subtle set of mechanisms that operate to support an inaccurate assumption and action consistent with it that this problem is one of the health of one child. The inefficiency of this chronic displacement as a mode of family adjustment becomes openly manifest with the development of the psychosis. At the same time the psychosis lends itself to being seen as a living confirmation of the accuracy of the assumption, and can become a focus for the perpetuation of the family mechanism.

NOTES

1. Paul Valery, *Dialogues* (Bollingen Series XLV, No 4) transl. by William Mc-Causland Stewart (New York: Pantheon, 1956). Permission to reproduce here is gratefully acknowledged.

2. The series considered is all the complete families with a schizophrenic son or daughter who participated in psychotherapy on the project.

The Family as the Unit of Study and Treatment Workshop, 1959
3. Image, Object, and Narcissistic Relationships
Warren M. Brodey, M.D. *
Guest Lecturer, Washington School of Psychiatry, Washington, D.C.
*Formerly Psychiatrist, Family Study Section, Clinical Investigations,
National Institute of Mental Health, Bethesda, Maryland.

In working with family units one sees modes of relationship which do not easily fit into the presently documented categories of relationship. One begins then to design categories which will be more sharply relevant to the broader application of the perspective gained. Let us begin by re-expanding a highly condensed summary developed in a previous report, "Some Family Operations and Schizophrenia" (1). There the following definition of the operations observed was made:

> Using the concept of externalization, the family operation observed can be defined thus: A network of narcissistic relationships, in which ego-dystonic aspects of self are externalized by each family member and regrouped into allegorical roles, each epitomizing a part of the major conflict which was acted out in the original marriage. These allegorical roles are played by family members, or by substitutes-others who have been induced into becoming overinvolved with the family conflict (2). The constellation of roles allows the internal conflict of each member to be acted out within the family, rather than within the self, and each family member attempts to deal with his conflicts by changing the other.

It is the purpose of this paper to present as clearly as possible the theoretical considerations that go into the above statement in their wider application. First let us review the concept externalization. Briefly stated, externalization is considered "a mechanism of defense defined as projection plus the *selective* use of reality for verification of the projection" (1).

Externalization as a major mechanism of defense takes on significance as one considers the second component—the selective use of reality for the verification of the projection. This selective use of reality was extreme in all the families observed, as well as the five families reported. Each family member appears to cathect with interest and meaningfulness only a limited aspect of his environmental surroundings—*that which validates expectation; the remainder of the reality available for perception is omitted.* Thus, within the family relationship each family member lives within a personal reality which has become constricted. The meaningful reality for use within the family relationships has become a series of stylized picture post cards; each snapshot is accurate but lacks the nuances of color, depth, and detail that give a sense of developing continuity—of unfolding yet to take place. *The ego-reality testing function is only partially maintained*: a logical system of viewing reality is built but, as stated, major elements of information are omitted from the testing process.

But no one can perceive all elements of reality at once. As Oppenheimer (3) states, one cannot be in all of the rooms of a house at once. And for each person, his perception of reality is indeed a small fragment of the total, and so it is for each succeeding generation. Each of us can look back to the proven assertions of the past and realize that their incorrectness often stemmed from what was not considered. How wonderful it is to be aware that there will always be the process of discovery to enhance the meanings and the attention that we give to the volley of stimuli which form the base material from which we build our thought images[1] of what lies within and beyond the boundaries of our own self-image.

The capacity of discover, to give meaning to and to value the unexpected is for each human important to survival; observation of the families studied has suggested *that the capacity to discover the unexpected, particularly as it signifies the beginnings of change, is reduced.* It is the axis of variability—variations in the capacity to discover the unexpected—that will be highlighted in contrasting the other and image relationships.

In the object relationship one's inner image of the person to whom one is related is maintained over time as a plastic replica of the other person as he exists within one's total experience. In the usual close relationship, one's inner image of the other person, even when he or she is at a distance, allows major prediction of the other's behavior. But as in a marriage, for example, there are always those moments when the other's performance is simply not related to what one has anticipated. To the extent that this unexpected behavior is discovered, given meaning and valued, a new aspect of the other's personality has emerged to be incorporated into the inner representation. This feedback between inner image and outer substantial reality allows the inner image of our loved one to grow and unfold.

What one expects has always much to do with what one is aware of, and how this is structured for predictive use. It is in terms *of the means of maintaining accurate prediction* that the image relationship is considered at the opposite extreme to the object relationship. *In the image relationship*, the inner image of the other person takes precedence: the emphasis is on *changing reality to fit with expectation* rather than expectation to fit reality. Accurate prediction is arduously maintained. The mother's image relationship to her child works at polarizing the child toward conforming to her mother's fantasy. The siblings of families studied have described entering into relationship with parents as entering into a powerful magnetic field, struggling to maintain identity, losing it to fulfill parent's expectations, relating then from within a restricted role now formalized into the family structure. To have relationship the sibling and other must fit each other's stereotyped image expectation. Discovery except as it verifies the expected is reduced.

But each of us seeks to integrate the world around him with his expectation; such integration is necessary for maintaining continuity. The category image relationship is reserved for those relationships at the end of the spectrum where the reality testing and prediction system specifically and profoundly operate to reduce the possibility of discovering aspects of the other's existence not fitting with the established expectation.

Let us focus for the moment on that which we do not anticipate in any way. This may be called "the unexpected." The *object relationship* uses the unexpected as a device for correcting the internal gestalt. The *image relationship* system uses the unexpected as a device for signaling the necessity to correct the outside world, or if this is not possible, to restrict what is perceived.

Now we return to the *narcissistic relationship*. This term has been in the paper "Some Family Operations and Schizophrenia" (1) to symbolize a way of relating defined briefly as: "a relationship with a projected or distanced part *of self* as mirrored in the behavior of another." Earlier in the paper at that point where the term is more fully defined, it is stated:

> As conceptualized, the narcissistic relationship includes two ingredients: one person relating to the other as a projected part of self, the fragment of self projected being un-integrated with either a perception of self or of the external object, and, second, the other person's becoming, within the specific relationship, symmetrical with the first person's expectations, validating them.

At this point I would consider that the briefer definition does not do justice to the concept of the narcissistic relationship. It is rather a part of the definition of the image relationship.[2]

The image and object relationships, as discussed, have been placed at the two ends of a linear continuum. The narcissistic relationship as defined does not fit along the same continuum. The narcissistic relationship is rather descriptive of two people *each making an image relationship to the other and each acting within this relationship so as to validate the image-derived expectation* of each other. Now we are moving toward a closed system. Both participants of the narcissistic relationship work at reducing the possibility of intrusions of the unexpected, using the devices of restriction and omission.

For the outsider looking into the narcissistic (family) relationship, the very neatness, consistency and pseudo logicalness can appear bizarre, but to the family it is a way of life (1). To the outsider the family appears captured within the constricting boundary of its reality. As one listens in therapy hours, one waits for those statements or actions which would reduce the predictable stereotypy which one observes. It is the psychotic member who seems to have found escape from the family prison of "realism." But his astonishingly perceptive comments are dismissed by the family as entirely crazy. The psychotic family member, met with the omission of any meaningfulness of his comment, may seek to establish more profoundly its now bizarre unexpectedness or in remission he may return to find identity in the restricted family role expected for him. Leaving psychosis may not mean health but only a return to the strait jacket of conforming with expectation. One patient while psychotic seemed alive, vibrant, and was most discerning in her relationship with the mother; but she was psychotic and her behavior unpredictable to the extreme. As she moved from this position back to what would be called by the mother "reasonableness," she returned to being a puppet dancing with every movement of her mother's hand with lifeless accuracy.[3] The road toward health transcends the dichotomy: bizarre and unexpected vs. complete conformity with others' expectations.

One more aspect of the narcissistic relationship seems significant to this presentation: in the narcissistic system of (family) relationships the unexpected is so reduced that each family member can predict how the other will behave within the family constellation. This being so, each member takes on a responsibility that most of us happily to large measure escape. Ordinarily, one can act for oneself—and leave to the other person the responsibility for taking his own position. But as the unexpected is removed and the system closed, each move would bring a known balancing and expected move from the other; then *one possesses a power of anticipation*, which gives one's acts new meaning as controlling the total balance. Operationally one becomes responsible for balancing others. Truly such a family becomes a single organism in more than a surface conceptual sense. As the family members observed so frequently expressed it, "Each family member *does* live for the other," and efforts to change self include the other family members. It is considered that the reduced use of the unexpected is an operational aspect of what has previously been called "phantasies of omnipotence."[4]

The above has been an effort to develop briefly some concepts that have been found useful in building a conception of family operation. In addition to further comments on externalization and the narcissistic relationship, an effort has been made to separate out the image relationship from the narcissistic relationship. The term narcissistic relationship is reserved for naming the between-two-persons reciprocal relationship as described above. The image relationship being a relationship-toward-a-person concept can be now appropriately defined in contradistinction to the object relationship.

Thus, in the object relationship the inner image of the object is being constantly redesigned to fit with the experience of the existing other; unexpected experiences are utilized for their corrective potential, broadening the relationship. In the image relationship, the inner image of the object is being used to constantly redesign the experience with the existing other, so that it will fit with inner determined prediction. The image relationship works toward omitting the unexpected, constricting the stereotyping of the relationship.

REFERENCES

1. Brodey, Warren M. *Some Family Operations and Schizophrenia: A Study of Fine Hospitalized Families Each with a Schizophrenic Member,* AMA Arch. Gen. Psychiatry, 1: 379–402, 1959.

2. Brodey, Warren M., and Marjorie Hayden. *Intrateam Reactions: Their Relation to the Conflicts of the Family in Treatment.* Am J. Orthopsychiatry, 27:349–355, 1957.

3. Oppenheimer, R. *Science and the Common Understanding.* New York: Simon and Schuster, 1954.

4. Adornto, T. W., et al. *The Authoritarian Personality.* New York: Harper, 1950.

5. Allport, Gordon W. *The Nature of Prejudice.* Boston: Beacon Press, 1954.

NOTES

1. Our images of the world inside and around us are not just thought. Each knows the sense of tension in his own arm as his favorite tennis player serves at a crucial point of the game.

2. It refers to developmental aspects of the image relationship: The image relationship is considered to have its roots in the process of relation to self as distanced to another. This stage budding out of primary narcissism precedes and potentiates the separation of the "me" from the "not-me." The later potential for cathexis of a "not-me other," which defines the object relationship, is an expression of the completeness of this separation process.

3. In Samuel Beckett's play *Waiting for Godot*, the theme "Is the capturer captured by his captive?" is pertinently symbolized in the roles of Pozzo and Lucky.

4. The problem of omnipotence and closed systems of philosophy—where all is neatly explainable and the possibility of divergence labeled ignorance—has received much attention in the social sphere. See Adorno and others (4) and Allport (5).

The Family as the Unit of Study and Treatment Workshop, 1959
4. The Emotional Life of the Family: Inferences for Social Casework,
Betty W. Basamania, M.S.S*
Natick, Massachusetts
*Formerly Psychiatric Social Worker, Family Study Section, Clinical Investigations, National Institute of Mental Health, Bethesda, Maryland.

Participation in the family project[1] offered an exceptional opportunity to observe, to study and to do therapy with the family as a unit. The dimension of the family unit which emerged during this study and became the focal interest of the project was that of the inner emotional life of the family. This is a dimension which has received less attention than other dimensions of the family, e.g., the social and the anthropological. In fact, it is a dimension that is difficult to bring into focus for oneself and equally difficult to communicate to others. Training and thinking have been oriented to the individual. Psychological theory and a conceptual system developed for the individual appear to have deterred observations of emotional phenomena in the family and psychological conceptualization of the family unit. It has followed that the clinical disciplines, e.g. psychiatry and social casework, have lacked the conceptual tools with which to do effective treatment with the family unit.

The research project offered an apt framework for the study of the emotional life of the family unit and for the development of an approach to the unit. The theoretical orientation regarded the schizophrenic problem as part of a process that involved the entire family. Systematic observations of family units were consistent with the hypothesis, and treatment, based upon these observations, was adapted to the family unit.

This paper will present a casework view of the project's particular approach to the family as a unit to illustrate the contribution such an approach can make toward the diagnosis and treatment of that unit. The approach was to regard the family unit as a single organism.[2]

In the following sections there will be a discussion of observations made as a result of seeing the family together, treatment of the family unit, and the inferences this approach has for social casework.

OBSERVATIONS

Observations included in this paper were selected on the basis of repetitive behavior manifestations, seen in each of the 11 families. The characteristics noted as significant within the families were also experienced by the staff in relating to the families. The observations were made as a result of seeing the family as a unit, and would have been much less clear, if not obscured, if family members had been seen individually. These observations were not all-inclusive of the data of this study but were outstanding in the effort to understand the functioning of these families with a particular kind of problem.

An examination of the observations showed that they could be grouped into clusters with similar theoretical or action characteristics. Observations in one category may have implications in another, but choice was made on the basis of the outstanding characteristic and related to the conceptual framework established on a theoretical or action basis. The two classifications are as follows: 1) Interrelated personality problems among family members, (a) ego identity problems, (b) reinforcement of ego deficits, (c) reciprocal support of ego defenses; 2) Interaction problems among family members,

(a) actions among family members, (b) communications among family members, (c) initiative among family members, (d) helplessness within the family in contrast to strength outside of it.

The first large classification, *interrelated personality problems among family members*, is woven upon a framework of psychological concepts concerning the individual and expanded to include the influence of the interwoven qualities of the unit. It may be questioned if the use of concepts appropriate to another unit (the individual) achieves maximum clarity and understanding about the phenomenon (the family) under study. I have chosen to make use of the concepts about the individual until family psychological concepts are formulated.

Ego identity problems were manifested in three notable areas, less definitively in others. First, confusion was shown in discriminating self from other members in the present family constellation.

In one family, the symptomatic daughter's behavior was volatile and vigorous and the vigorousness increased rapidly in proportion to her anxiety. The mutual attachment between this young woman and her mother was an intense one. It was possible to observe, repeatedly, a sequence which started with an emotional outburst on the daughter's part and which was followed by the revelation that the mother had been exceedingly anxious over a particular situation. The daughter's behavior reflected the mother's feelings sooner than did the mother's behavior. At another time, when this mother's defense of overadequacy was shaken by a need for nursing care postoperatively, she was intensely concerned that her nonsymptomatic daughter would become schizophrenic. In actuality, this daughter's adjustment was stable. The husband in this family said that his wife was an anxiety generator from whom he took on anxiety. He had a marked problem in identifying his own anxiety and distinguishing it from his wife's anxiety.

Second, parental personality problems were projected upon their offspring.

One father, with an advanced educational background, could not come to grips about anything with his symptomatic son. He expressed fear that "the worst might happen" if he were firm with his son, and then elaborated on criminal instincts, defects and antisocial behavior of psychotics. The son's symptoms were ritualistic obsessions and withdrawal. The fantasy fears behind the father's passivity were talked about as possibilities for the son.

Third, the mothers showed confused identification of past family figures with the symptomatic offspring. In their fantasy, the mothers identified their offspring with family figures about whom the mother had cause to be anxious: e.g., a sickly father who died; sickly sisters who "took all the grandmother's time to keep alive"; a brother who became psychotic; the death of siblings of the child.

One mother described the maternal grandfather to her symptomatic son by saying that he was not sociable and that she was that way as a child too. She said, "It is said children are more like the grandparents than parents. Of course, he died of pneumonia." At this point, the son's arms started an involuntary shaking. She went on to tell how relatives died of tuberculosis, and about family pilgrimages to the west seeking a climate to combat "coughs," "passing out" and other somatic afflictions. The climax came when the grandfather got wet and developed a cough which went into pneumonia or malaria. She said that her son must be a lot like him and that she had fainting spells like her father. She continued to elaborate on how genes "double and redouble," and since her husband's grandmother was odd, their son got it, doubled and redoubled.

There was *reinforcement of ego deficits* among the family members. The fact that most of the families in the study had attained success in business or in a profession contrasted to the ineffectual functioning of these members within their families. A principle of extremes characterized the family functioning: e.g., all-none; dependence-independence; aggression-passivity; omnipotence-helplessness; right-wrong. Perceptions appeared to be made in terms of these emotional extremes.

The parents in one family ran a business. When they were together there was a constant struggle between them over who was to be the boss. If the husband tried to be the boss, the wife presented that she was degraded and humiliated in an inferior position. When the wife undertook the boss position, the husband withdrew from the business and did nothing. In actuality, both the husband and the wife were capable in their business. While one parent appeared to be the superadequate person, the other would seem to be helpless; at times they shifted in these positions, revealing the common base for both extremes.

There was another characteristic which resulted in inefficient functioning in the family. This was the lack of integration between cognition and action; there was a disparity between what one said and what one did.

In one family, the mother declared that the children should learn to take responsibility, but despite having five teen-age children, she would require nothing of them by way of household duties. The father berated the children for not helping their mother and for being irresponsible about money but he refused them an allowance or any part in financial matters.

There was *reciprocal support of ego defenses* among the family members. The problems of the family were discussed as though they belonged to the symptomatic member and that member had a propensity for accepting the offerings. The symptomatic member was designated as "the sick one," "the one," "the helpless or stupid one," "the crazy or the schizophrenic one." The designation selected for "the patient" by a particular family had its counterpart in the family problem. In the family in which the central struggle between the parents was the overadequate-inadequate issue, the symptomatic daughter acted like a helpless little child, even to speaking in a high-pitched childish voice, and the parents treated her as though she were helpless.

The families found it difficult to define their problems. This was an area in which support of one another's defenses contributed to inefficient functioning.

> One of the families was concerned and anxious lest the symptomatic member leave the therapy program. At the therapy session, the father talked all around this problem; his wife made one attempt by saying, "We're talking around the bush," but when her husband responded with a reference to his anxiety, she retreated. The next day, the father headed into the problem and his wife directed with anxious details on unrelated subjects.

In a similar way, the wives and husbands were "protective" of one another in that neither introduced anxiety-provoking discussion and much energy was expended in maintaining the *status quo*. If the wife raised a question about her relationship with her husband, she added one about their offspring; he picked up on the latter and ignored the former. The husband expressed concern to say "the right thing" to his wife and felt if he said what he wanted, he would be "like a mouse in a hole." Their symptomatic son said that he always talked individually with his father or with his mother; somehow, what he said to one was not suitable to say to the other. The father and mother had equal difficulty in carrying out a three-way discussion.

The second large classification, *interaction problems among family members,* is one that cannot be directly observed without seeing the family members together. In working with individuals, much is deduced about how the individual interacts with his family from what he says, from theoretical knowledge about him, and from the way in which he related to the therapist. Having lacked much direct evidence of how a family functions in action, this area is a particularly fruitful one for further study.

When the family members on this project were seen together in therapy and the orientation was toward the family unit, a striking *patterns of action* came into view. The family members did not deal with one another; instead, they turned to the therapist, whom they wished to cast as "the expert." The parents wanted to tell the therapist about their offspring's problems while the young adult was sitting beside them; marital partners complained about one another to the therapist while each was present. This same pattern operated outside of therapy as well; family members turned to nurses and other staff members rather than to deal directly with their family. The higher the anxiety and tension in the family, the more members turned to the outside, as though the tension decreased with distance. A variation of this pattern was to have the threesome (father, mother, grown child) function and relate to one another in pairs; each twosome discussed problems they had with the missing third member but the twosome did not deal with problems between them.

There was evidence that the problems in *communications among the family members* had been of long standing.

One family, after their first three weeks on the study, exclaimed over the family affairs they were hearing about for the first time, after 30 years of marriage. The wife said she had been unable to reach her husband; she tried to tell him when the family needed money, when she was sick and needed an operation, when arrangements had to be made to attend a relative's funeral—but her husband never listened; he was always in a hurry to be off to his important job. The husband explained that he was from a healthy family and he couldn't understand his wife's habitual ailments. In therapy he wanted to discuss these problems and to reach a better understanding with his family. The wife noticed that she could talk about their problems in the therapy meetings while at home her voice became so shrill that her husband departed before discussions began. After the husband talked about big arguments that he had over little things with his wife, the symptomatic son responded to his father by saying, "And you tell me not to let little things bother me; I've seen you upset by little things many times."

In the family atmosphere of "jammed" communications, secrets were maintained between some members which excluded others, and particular matters, albeit innocuous in reality content, were *verboten* subjects for discussion.

One mother attempted to keep any issue concerning her son from discussion in the therapy meetings on the basis that "you will hurt him." When the matter of discussing difference in front of the son became an issue between the mother and the father, it was learned, next, that the mother solved this problem by influencing the son not to attend therapy meetings. This same father shared his son's sexual and omnipotence fantasies and promised not to tell the mother. After the parents shared their concern over the fantasies, the son questions whether the father kept the secret and the parents maintained that he did so. The father accounted for the commitment to the secret on the basis of keeping his son's confidence.

Initiative often appeared to be lacking when the families tried to arrive at a decision upon which action could be taken. This resulted in a paradoxical turn to the interaction among the family members. The father and mother disagreed on what the other wished to do; a state of paralysis ensued until the symptomatic member moved in, and thus made the decision.

One family spent several hours trying to decide what to visit on a sight-seeing tour. The son became impatient at waiting to depart while the parents debated their destination. By the time the family got underway, the son decided that he wouldn't go, the mother made a brief effort to be firm about the departure, the father did nothing and the family remained at home.

The *helplessness* of the father in the above episode characterized his *functioning in the family*. In contrast he has been *highly capable in his work.* His positions have entailed administrative responsibility for a program which required initiative and original thinking as well as working effectively with people. The mother had a college education but presented herself as uninformed and lacking in capabilities, although she has accomplished as much as the average woman in her socioeconomic group. She emphasized that she was extra-sensitive and extra-fragile.

THERAPY

Therapy has been an integral part of the research project. It has been one of the sources for observation and a method for testing the hypothesis that the schizophrenic symptoms in one member are a part of a process in the family. An additional interest has been to adapt therapeutic methods to the treatment of the family as a unit. This latter aspect is particularly pertinent to social casework. This paper will discuss some of the experiences and ways that have been found useful in working with these families.

The philosophy underlying therapy and the attitudes which stem from the philosophy are the substance out of which therapy is conducted. The philosophy on the project was based upon a regard for the family and its capacity to nurture human growth. Therapeutically, a guiding principle was to respond to the families in a way that would promote growth. For example, the families continued as many of their usual responsibilities as was possible in a hospital setting. This included the family's being responsible for their symptomatic member and using nursing staff if they needed to help with this family function. If staff were to take over the families, making the family decisions and planning for them, dependency would be increased and the use of capacities impaired.

Flexibility was necessary to adapt treatment to an evolving and expanding knowledge about the families on the project. The observations were the source for the enrichment of understanding the psychological forces within the family. Therapeutic changes were made in response to the increased understanding and the continual clinical experience with the families. With this general background about therapy, let us turn to other therapeutic aspects of a more specific nature.

The interaction problems within the families have been approached through "action" on the therapist's part; that is, through the therapeutic structure the therapist maintained. For example, it was necessary to have more than one family member presenting the interviews if therapy was to be done with the family as a unit. Concerned and anxious families decrease tension with distance rather than with unity and this phenomenon was manifested in the attendance, or lack of it, of family members at therapy interviews. It was found possible to work with two members of the family but more profitable to work with three. The presence of two members was made a minimum requirement for the therapy interviews.

Another action on the therapist's part was to refrain from interfering with the family's interaction. The word "action" emphasizes the difference between doing it and talking about the advisability of family interaction. To accomplish this, a therapist may need to check on his own anxieties in tension-laden situations and about open conflict. A therapist would have difficulty allowing a family to work on their problems if he feared stress, open conflict and anxiety.

The therapist's verbalized observations about the way the family was or was not interacting was often sufficient to mobilize the family's efforts to increase direct interaction. This automatically increased the communication among family members and, usually, it appeared to be a reassuring experience. It served to dispel fantasy fears, i.e., that the other member could not sustain verbalization, and the participants learned that the anxiety was tolerable and could be dealt with. After talking with one another, one family member might express surprise that another member received his pronouncement so calmly, and describe his fear, previously, at saying what he had on his mind. Or, after an intense exchange, relief was expressed, and often, a feeling of accomplishment. Some of the families had an abundance of verbal exchange but their communication problem was as great as those who had little. When these families were able to talk together without obliterating each exchange by the feelings expressed, their communication system began to function. This usually occurred when the family had moved to the point where members could talk more about themselves and less about how the other members should change.

Observations made by the therapist about family interaction brought family patterns of behavior into their awareness, opening areas they could work upon in therapy. These behavioral patterns were frequently the outward manifestation of basic personality problems within the family. For example, the families were as unaware that it was often the symptomatic member who made the family decisions as they were of their unconscious projection upon him. They were surprised when the therapist noted the reality situation, such as the decision-making, as it occurred in the family. The problem behind the lack of decision-making action was that the parents had no stand of their own. In this dilemma, they sought and followed any authority within reach. They read an article by an expert who advised patience and they followed this, regardless of how unrealistic and ridiculous the results. The family's awareness of their behavior was a first step in their effort to unfold the layers of the underlying problem.

An understanding of the interrelated personality problems among these family members opened areas for treatment. Observations about the ego identity problems among the family members led to a more acute awareness on their part of when one member infringed upon another. The confusions, inherent in ego identity problems, could then be dealt with therapeutically with increased clarity. In turn, family members gained awareness of "whose backyard" they were operating in and were able to speak for themselves. With the symptomatic member accepting the family projections upon him, a therapist unfamiliar with this process might accept the projection as fact and thus reinforce its effects. Not accepting the projections, which may be more in attitude than in literal verbalization, allies the therapist with reality rather than with the fantasy and the feelings of the family.

In a similar way, when the pattern of extremes within the family was recognized, the fact that there was a broad expanse of middle ground containing many choices and possibilities was more obvious and the therapist was not persuaded that situations were as impossible as the family felt them to be. There was another important aspect to understanding the way in which the family's perception, made in terms of emotional extremes, affected their relationships, including those with the therapist. If the family was one in which right-wrong prevailed, they perceived the therapist was judging them as right or wrong regardless of whether this was so. They framed questions and carried on discussion in these terms and the therapist could find himself on the end of one of the extremes when this was not his intention.

When the family became aware of the discrepancies between their actions and their words, another door was opened if they wished to see what they could do to change. This characteristic is not different from other contradictions which signal that the irrational holds sway over the rational, but it is one which is difficult to see taking place in therapy unless the family is seen together.

When a reciprocal support of defenses took place between two people, or among more than two, it was possible for the therapist to interpret the defense in terms of the family interaction. This was on a different level than most interpretations of a defense made by the therapist to the individual in therapy. The therapist's interpretation became something that two or more family members worked upon together in contrast to the individual working on an interpretation about himself with a person who is usually seen as an authoritative figure. This is a definitive example which has implications in broader areas of therapeutic interest. There were changes in the area of the patient-therapist relationship[3] and in transference and countertransference when therapy was conducted with the family as a unit.

In working therapeutically with the family as a unit there was a shift from the intrapsychic problems of the individual to the dynamic interplay of problems among the members of the family unit. From the family's standpoint, since all members were present in therapy, shifts went on simultaneously among the members of the unit.

In individual therapy the individual discusses his problems with the therapist and interaction is between these two. In family therapy the family's problems are discussed and interacted upon, largely, by the family members. Each family member is affected by the family problems. The family may act as though the problems belong to only one member, but if that member takes action, verbal or otherwise, he can engage other family members. When more members become engaged in finding a solution to the problems, the ensuing interaction and verbalization become a "working through process," one in which each member comes to have a better view of his contribution to the problems and can then contribute more to their solution. The family members are the persons who will be living together when therapy is ended. Learning to work together in finding solutions is an ongoing family function. From the observations on the project, the member who clings to the problems as if they were his only is the symptomatic member. Problems may be discussed with each member disclaiming his part in them, or with so little vigor that members become weary and doubtful of their ability to deal with the problems. The therapist's observations or interpretations on what is taking place in the family at such times can help the family to get under way again.

These examples illustrate the alteration in the usual patient-therapist relationship when therapy was directed at the family as a unit. In the experience of the project, the therapist could not establish one-to-one relationships with individual members in the family unit and have therapy effective. To identify with one member the therapist runs the risk of being against another member, and he has made a place for himself in the family group. This is a difficult position from which to be helpful to the family. It complicates the factors with which the family is trying to deal and increases the possibility for the therapist to project his feelings and values on the family. A high degree of self-awareness was needed for the therapist to maintain an objective position from which to understand what was taking place in the family, and not be caught up in the emotional processes actually going on among the family members in the therapy sessions. The therapist does not judge nor make demands of the family but he tries to be clear on his own position and to communicate this explicitly through the therapy structure to the family.

The therapist distinguishes between factual and feeling content expressed by the family. In families with a psychotic problem, feelings are intense and anxieties are at a high level. The anxiety may be overtly expressed in action or it may be covertly reflected by immobility and blocking. When anxiety is high, reality becomes distorted. The therapist not only needs to be aware of the anxiety in the family, but also needs to distinguish between "what is" and what the family feels to be so. From this reality base, the therapist allies himself with the capabilities in the family. The deeply meaningful feelings attached to family relationships are expressed among the family members in therapy and the therapist does not interfere with such expression. The therapist desires to stay out of the position which would say he has the answers to the family's problems, that he is "the expert," that he is stronger and more capable than the family.

Transference and countertransference are present in therapy with the family unit but can be diluted. When the parents are present for the offspring in therapy and the marital pair are present for one another, transference to the therapist can be reduced. The therapist could change this by intervening but the minimization of transference is seen as valuable in utilizing family capabilities. The regressive aspects of transference are theoretically established, as Miss Garrett has pointed out: "Since regressive feelings always occur in transference and countertransference, it tends to be the child in the adult client with whom the worker identifies. He tends to react to the child in the client as a child himself. In such cases unconscious regressive childish attitudes dominate client and worker."[4]

Countertransference in the therapist is present in family therapy as it is in individual therapy. The therapist has been a member of a family, and may bring unrecognized patterns from his own family just as he brings other attitudes and feelings into therapy. However, the position of the therapist, outlined above, would tend to dilute countertransference also. There is an additional factor that has implications not only for countertransference and transference but for the entire process of doing therapy with more than the individual. This is the difficulty which is encountered in relating to more than one individual at a time. If the observation in these families has broader application, it is much easier to relate in one-to-one relationships than among three or more people.

The observations made on the families in the hospital setting were of greater value in learning about the families than those made on families in the outpatient setting, but the latter families moved forward more readily in therapy. This outcome seemed due to factors intrinsic to a hospital setting, such as complexities arising out of staff-family relationships and the protective and authoritative aspects of hospitals which tend to foster dependency in patients.

INFERENCE FOR SOCIAL CASEWORK

There is broad interest in social casework in developing theory and concepts appropriate to the family. Much of the current effort has been directed at the integration of sociological concepts with casework practice. The dimension of the emotional life of the family has been less clearly delineated.

Caseworkers have undertaken therapy with marital partners or with a combination of family members and have encountered a variety of problems. Often, the problems obscured advantages that could stem from therapy with the family unit. This has resulted in some caseworkers' becoming adherents to an individual therapeutic approach only. On the other hand, further study of the factors involved in the two approaches may make possible the identification of specific factors which influence the effectiveness of each approach.

There are differences between the casework approach to the individual and therapy with the family unit. The primary difference would be the shift from the relationship between the therapist and the individual to that between the therapist and a unit composed of several members. To clarify the meaning of this shift involves theoretical consideration of the therapeutic relationship. Definitions of the casework relationship with the client vary. Some would include the caseworker as a parent surrogate and would have the caseworker offer an object relationship in which the client identifies with the ego strengths in the therapist. Neither of these facets would be appropriate to the therapist's relationship with the family unit. In family unit therapy, the therapist aims at maintaining the original family relationship within the family unit. The potentials for growth are seen as being in the family and the therapist's aim is to enable the family to develop these potentialities. This position may not be as satisfying to some therapists as the individual relationship, depending upon one's emotional motivation for being in the therapist's role.

Therapy with the family unit opened areas for treatment. Therapeutic work with the interaction problems noted in the observations is different from therapeutic work with the individual or therapeutic group work. It signals an area that has not been available to utilize in treatment. It is interesting that work on these problems could be facilitated by action on the therapist's part which often related to the therapeutic structure he maintained. The usual casework methods make use of the expression of feeling, of verbalization and thinking, but little use of action. The discrepancies between actions and words, observed in the families, would suggest the need for the development of additional therapeutic methods. Other recent research has pointed out how verbal communication, one of the tools of casework, is limited in usefulness in attempts to establish therapeutic relationships with particular types of families.[5]

There are factors in family unit therapy, as described here, which offer opportunities to assess ego strengths and to do therapeutic work at an ego level. More of the individual member's ego is seen in action as family members work together on the problems they have in relating to one another, and through the ways in which they deal with everyday living situations. Therapeutic work on underlying personality problems can begin at the family's behavioral and action level. The dilution of the transference and counter-transference does not encourage regressive tendencies in the family and in the therapist.

It is an opinion that social caseworkers have felt more confidence in working with families when the problem was not a psychotic one. Perhaps it is due to the vagueness which may be matched by the subtle nature of the manifestations of the psychotic problem. An example of the difference in the social work approach to the psychotic and nonpsychotic problems might be reflected in the following two observations. The family's projection of family problems onto the psychotic member has not been widely noted while the observation of this mechanism is fairly commonplace when the problem is a neurotic one.

The observations and treatment of these families bring additional perspective to some usual areas in casework practice. The caseworker may unwittingly add to the communication problems in the family. He may become the keeper of one member's secrets from another member. The dynamic psychological problem becomes obscured by the social work ethic concerned with confidentiality. When working with the family as a unit, it can be established early in therapy that the therapist will not participate in keeping secrets and that any communication to him from one member may be conveyed to the other members.

The observations showed how family members often do not distinguish between their own anxiety and the anxiety of other members. This observation might profitably be explored in the caseworker-client relationship. A question could be raised as to whether, in the caseworker's empathy with his client, he may, at times, take on the client's anxiety. By so doing, the caseworker becomes more susceptible to the reality distortions which stem from the anxiety and he is less able to be helpful to the client. For example, the caseworker would be more easily convinced that the client's feelings of helplessness and inadequacy were actually so despite the client's strengths and capabilities. This is not a fertile base from which to utilize the client's ego strengths in casework treatment.

The family unit approach could alter some of the familiar therapeutic problems in casework. The natural dependence of children on their parents would not be interrupted as it is, at times, with the individual approach. Insecure parents would not be threatened by the therapist who sees their child alone, nor one marital partner by the other partner's relationship with the caseworker. There would be more opportunity for the changes in the adjustment of various family members to take place simultaneously than when one member is in therapy or when family members are seen individually by different therapists. There would no longer be such questions as: Which member of the family should be seen in treatment? In what sequence? Which therapist should see which family member?

With the renewed interest in casework diagnostic and therapeutic approaches to the family, a frequent question is, which cases should be approached on an individual basis, and which on a family basis? This seems to me to be a precipitate question. Much work would need to be done with the family as a unit to have adequate data on which to base conceptualization, to develop classifications concerning the family unit, and to establish diagnoses for family problems. One such question might ask if the family unit approach would be appropriate with young children, and if so, at what ages? The offspring on the project are young adults. Other studies are being done which use a similar approach with families who have a different type of problem and different-aged children. An aggregate of studies or experiences in practice using this approach could supply data which, when studied systematically, could give valid answers.

In summary, the family as a unit approach can offer data toward the formulation of a family diagnosis, and opens additional possibilities for treatment. It makes possible a broad use of therapeutic work to be done at the ego level and opens areas for the support of the capacities and strengths within the family unit.

NOTES

*Permission to reprint is gratefully acknowledged by Dr. Bowen and the staff of the Family Study Project. "The Family as a Unit of Study and Treatment Workshop." First Published in the *American Journal of Orthopsychiatry* Vol. 31.1, pages 40–86. John Wiley & Sons.

1. The project was conducted at the National Institute of Mental Health, U.S. Public Health Service, Bethesda, Maryland.
2. The term "organism" is used according to the dictionary definition: "any highly complex thing-with parts so integrated that their relation to one another is governed by their relation to the whole."

3. The "patient-therapist relationship" is used in the broad sense to be interchangeable with "client-caseworker relationships."

4. Annette Garrett, The Worker-Client Relationship, Am J. Orthopsychiatry, 19:224–238, 1949.

5. Charlotte S. Henry, Motivation in Non-voluntary Clients, Soc. Casework., 39: 130–136, 1958.

6

The Prospectus
A Project Summary

INTRODUCTION

Family Research Project for the Study and Treatment of Schizophrenic Patients and Their Families is a comprehensive summary of the Family Study Project written after the project ended for a grant that unfortunately never materialized (Bowen, 1959). It is the best summary about the project located in the Bowen Archives.

In it, Bowen first presents an overview of the project. He also describes the two phases of the research—the first year, and the second phase that lasted the final three years. After the first year, the orientation was changed to the family as an emotional unit. While a conventional individual focus was favored by the administration, the research staff fortunately chose a family orientation. It was at that time that parents and siblings of the patient were included in the research effort.

At the end of 1955, "the hypothesis was changed from one which saw the schizophrenic psychosis as a phenomenon in one person, to one which regarded the psychosis in the patient as a symptom of an active process that involved every member of the family" (Bowen, 1959, p. 6).

Bowen noted that the shift from an individual to a family orientation required three challenging steps. First, the staff had to think in terms of treating the family; second, they had to relate to the family rather than the individual; last, the family had to be treated as a single unit. These were not (and are not today) easy steps.

The concept of the family as an emotional unit—and its derivative, family psychotherapy—were utilized for the final three years of the study. Interestingly, each psychotherapy hour was tape recorded, and the staff made daily written summaries. The transcription and analysis of these tapes would be a future project in and of itself.

Bowen summarizes the major results of the Family Study Project in five areas. First, there was the specification of the concept of "the family as a unit" as the primary finding. Second, various family behavioral patterns were described through the lens of the family as an emotional unit. Third, family psychotherapy was developed and refined for "the family as a unit." Fourth, a family theory of schizophrenia was developed. Last, there was the often overlooked but important finding of the interaction between emotional and physical symptoms. One of the staff psychiatrists, Dr. Brodey, served as the primary care physician for the families during the last three years of the research, and a significant relationship between emotional and physical symptoms was observed.

THE PROSPECTUS—A PROJECT SUMMARY

Family Research for the
Study and Treatment of Schizophrenic
Patients and Their Families

This prospectus will describe an unusual clinical psychiatric research project which was conducted at the National Institute of Mental Health, Bethesda, Maryland from November 1, 1954 to January 1, 1959. A foundation grant is sought to finance the writing of a detailed report about this research work.

Project Background

The project was one of the first formal psychiatric studies started in the newly opened Clinical Center at the National Institutes of Health. The project occupied a new ward that had never been used. In the beginning, the Institution had a very idealistic research philosophy which encouraged and supported new and imaginative research that would not be possible in less well endowed institutions. This attitude and unusual setting provided the incentive for the staff to go all out in theoretical thinking, and for the Institution to go all out in supporting the effort. This project probably would never have been possible under other circumstances. There was a full time research staff of three psychiatrists, one social worker and two research assistants; a ward staff of 12 to 15 consultants and observers who represented psychiatry, psychoanalysis, psychology, sociology, anthropology and other disciplines. The total four year investment represented an estimated 80 man years of staff time and a total cost of almost one million dollars. Murray Bowen, M.D. was the originator and director of the project. Other members of the medical staff were Robert H. Dysinger, M.D. and Warren M. Brodey, M.D.

The research plan was one which required the "normal" parents to live on the ward and to participate in the treatment program with the patient. This plan was designed to explore an area of crucial theoretical and practical importance in psychiatry. On a practical level, there had been previous clinical experience, in the treatment of patients and parents separately, to suggest that treatment results could be more favorable than in the more conventional setting. On a theoretical level, this would permit direct observation of the parent in a continuing living situation with the patient. Most of our psychological theories have been developed from the psychoanalyst's detailed analysis of the individual patient. In spite of efforts to be objective, and to secure data from other sources, the analyst's main source of data is the patient, and the theory comes to see the family through the eyes of the patient. In this context it is easy for the theory to see the parents as the "cause" and to "blame" them for the patient's problem, and to see the patient as the innocent "victim" of a "cold dominating mother and a passive weak father."

The original research hypothesis had been developed from long experience in psychotherapy with schizophrenic patients, and also with their parents. The theoretical thinking had been based on the generally accepted psychoanalytic principles which regarded the schizophrenia as a psychopathological entity within the person of the patient, which had developed in the child's very early relationship with the mother. Our clinical experience agreed with the predominant trend in the literature which considered the mother to be the central figure in the patient's problem. The hypothesis considered the mother-patient relationship to be an intense interdependency, described in the literature as "symbiotic." The symbiotic relationship was seen as one initiated by the infant's automatic response to emotional immaturity in the mother, as an involvement that neither wanted, and as a situation against which both had struggled unsuccessfully over the years. At least the original hypothesis had made one step toward dealing with the "cause" and "blame" dilemma.

Three severely impaired schizophrenic patients and their mothers participated in the project during the first year in a "trial run" effort. The initial research design was:

1. Mother and patient to live together on the ward.
2. Staff to avoid directing or influencing the course of events between the mothers and patients. According to the hypothesis, this would provide more objective observations as well as facilitate psychotherapy.

3. Provide each mother and each patient with a psychotherapy relationship designed to permit each to grow toward maturity and to resolve the attachment to each other.

The results of the first year were as follows:

1. It WAS possible to create a ward environment in which mothers and patients voluntarily and enthusiastically continued the living together situation. Many hundreds of hours of staff time went into the creation of the ward environment. It is doubtful that the mothers could have remained for long if the theoretical thinking had "blamed" the mothers.
2. There was excellent agreement between the actual research observations and the predictions made by the hypothesis. Behavior, relationship patterns, and clinical course of the mothers and patients had been predicted from the hypothesis.
3. There were some areas of observation which had not been predicted and which were completely unexpected. The research now focused on the unexpected. Much will be said about this later. Briefly, the hypothesis had been based on work with mothers and patients individually, or from working with them together for brief periods. We had correctly predicted the way each, as an individual, would relate to the other, as an individual. We had not anticipated the new order of things revealed in the con*stant living together* situation. There was an "emotional oneness" between mother and patient in which, in terms of feelings, thoughts and fantasies, the two could "be as one." This was quite different from the "emotional separateness" between a mother and her normal child. In addition, there were definite characteristics to the way this "mother-patient oneness" related to those outside the "oneness," such as other family members and ward staff. The mechanisms in the mother were a direct "mirror image" opposite of mechanisms in the patient. In a sense, the personality structure of one really could not exist without the complementing opposite characteristics in the other. In addition, the mother-child "oneness" did not have the characteristics of a phenomenon conformed to two people. It appeared to be a shifting fragment of a larger family system. From observation we knew this "oneness" could attach itself to other family members. Our experience led us to hypothesize that the father was intimately involved, and the entire family could be involved.
4. The mothers and patients utilized individual psychotherapy to the point that emotional friction between them was alleviated. Neither went on toward emotional detachment from each other, as had been hypothesized. This was further evidence of the intensity of the "oneness."

Second Phase

At the end of one year, the theoretical orientation was changed to the "family as a unit" hypothesis. At this point the research could have gone in either of two directions. We could have retained the conventional orientation and focused on the individual and his relationship to other individuals in the family, or we could change the focus to the family "oneness." We had the research facility to make an exploration into this different way of thinking and there were observations to support the family hypothesis as a profitable way to approach the problem. The research administration favored a continuation of the individual orientation but agreed to support the project staff into the family exploration.

At the end of 1955, the hypothesis was changed from one which saw the schizophrenic psychosis as a phenomenon in one person, to one which regarded the psychosis in the patient as a symptom of an active process that involved every member of the family. A project paper published in March, 1958 was entitled "The Patient Is The Family." Just as a generalized disease in a single person can focus on and disable a single part of the family organ, so a generalized family illness can focus on and disable a single part of the family organism. The research plan was changed to permit entire family units (father, mother, patient, normal siblings) to live together on the ward. Small families were chosen in which the hypothesized problem would be contained within a small group of people. The ward milieu was changed from individual to family unit orientation. For instance, occupational therapy was adapted to family activity rather than individual. The parents assumed the principal responsibility for the care of the psychotic family member. Individual psychotherapy was discontinued and a "family psychotherapy" was started. All family members attended all psychotherapy hours together. "Family psychotherapy" proved to be extremely beneficial. It has since become rather widely accepted as one of the promising new developments in psychiatry. Each year, numbers of new psychotherapists are experimenting with different versions of the approach. The staff of this project has played a major role in the development of "family psychotherapy."

The shift from the individual to the family unit orientation involved three major steps. The first required the staff to THINK in terms of the family rather than the individual. There was no precedent for this way of thinking. All psychological theories, terminology, diagnostic categories, literature, and teaching is based on the familiar orientation which regards the individual as the unit of illness. It was difficult for staff to give up the "second nature" individual orientation, and easy to revert to it. The use of a familiar term of diagnostic label, associated with the individual, was sufficient to cause an automatic reversion from family unit to individual thinking. To facilitate the shift to family unit thinking we avoided the use of familiar psychiatric terms and used simple descriptive words. The second step was to RELATE to the family as a unit rather than to individuals in the family. It was not possible to RELATE to the family as a unit until there had been success in the THINKING step. There were multiple resistances to this second step. First, there were the resistance in the staff. There were also constant automatic forces in the family to individualize the family problem and to fix it in the weakest one by "blaming," attaching diagnostic labels, and using terms like "sick," "incompetent," "stupid," and "patient." Each family member attempted to force the therapist to agree with his or her individual viewpoint. There were forces in the hospital environment to oppose the family orientation. Every hospital has a strict administrative structure based on the concept of the individual as the unit of illness. Hospital structure requires the designation "patient" and that the illness in the individual be named with a diagnosis. It required considerable flexibility and working together with the Institution for the project to exist in the hospital environment of the Clinical Center. The third step was to TREAT the family psychotherapeutically as a single unit. The third step was not possible until there had been some measure of success at the first two steps.

The "family unit" hypothesis and "family psychotherapy" were used the remaining three years of the research study. The three original mother-patient families continued in the study, and additional eight families with fathers lived on the ward an average of one year each, and six father-mother-patient families were treated in outpatient family psychotherapy. The fathers could work in town as long as they arranged to attend the daily family psychotherapy hours. There is voluminous research data. Every psychotherapy hour was tape recorded. In addition there were three simultaneous written records of each hour. One observer made a summary of the content of the hours, another made a set of process psychotherapy notes, and a third observer made a process sociogram. The nursing staff made detailed observations on each family member, and on each family unit for the 24-hour period of each day. Research assistants have abstracted much of the voluminous data into daily, weekly and monthly summaries. All the written data has been made available to the project staff for any future writing. The 2,000 tape recordings are the property of the National Institute of Mental Health. The Institute has agreed to store them for two years and to lend them for research study during the two years, or to exchange them for new tapes if the former staff is able to finance a detailed research report.

Results of the Study

This project far exceeded the highest expectations of those who designed and carried out the study. The inductive method was used, rather than the more popular deductive method which has now come to be used almost exclusively by the basic sciences. The inductive method, the one used by Freud and Pavlov, was used to focus on a broad clinical area and to utilize "emergent" findings to determine the course of the research. At the beginning of the study, there was no way to guess that the "family unit" hypothesis and "family psychotherapy" would emerge as a central theme of the study.

Once it was possible for the staff to THINK about, to RELATE to, to TREAT, and to SEE the family as a unit rather than a collection of individuals, a whole new dimension of clinical observation came into view. We have compared this to shifting a microscope from an oil immersion to a low power lens, or to moving from the playing field to the top of the stadium to watch a football game. Once it was possible to get a broader perspective, to defocus the individual, and to get the entire family into the field of vision at once, it was possible to see broad patterns of form and movement that had been obscured by the close-up view of the individual. The family view in no way detracts from the importance of the familiar individual orientation. Instead, just as a view through an oil immersion lens can be more meaningful after a view through the low power lens, so the individual orientation can be more meaningful after it has been possible to see family patterns.

More specifically, the major results of this research have been:

1. Definition and elaboration of the theoretical concept "the family as a unit."
2. Description of family patterns of behavior that came into view after it was possible to see "the family as a unit," rather than a group of individuals.
3. Systematic development of the methodology and techniques of psychotherapy for "the family as a unit."
4. Development of a family theory of schizophrenia.

In the following section, each of these points will be described in more detail:

1. *The Concept of "The Family as a Unit."* A general notion of his concept has been presented in the preceding pages. On an intellectual level, the shift from the individual to the family unit orientation would appear to be simple and obvious. On a clinical level, the shift has subtle and far reaching implications that involve a major change in the theory and practice of medicine, and in the way man thinks about himself and illness. It is hard to arrive at the family unit orientation but, when this is possible, a whole new area of theoretical and clinical possibility comes into view. In reviewing the literature, we have found one other study in which the "family unit" orientation was clearly

presented. This is in a book published in 1944, "Patients Have Families," by Dr. Henry B. Richardson, an internist at Cornell Medical School. The book reports a long term interdisciplinary study on psychosomatic problems. Sections of the book are headed, "The Family as the Unit of Illness" and "The Family as the Unit of Treatment." He used the following kind of an example from a medical history to illustrate a point: There was a chief complaint of menstrual irregularity, a family history that the mother had died of diabetes in 1954, and a present illness that the menstrual problem began 5 years ago. The data had been compartmentalized in the record, and in the thinking of the doctors. The record showed no recognition that the menstrual problem began the year the mother died or that there might have been some relatedness between the mother's death and the daughter's symptoms. As far as is known, Richardson did not attempt to use the theoretical idea in a clinical operation, nor did he do any further writing about the concept.

In the past few years there has been an increasing number of family research studies. Terms like "the family," "the family unit," and "the family as a unit" have become commonplace. These terms denote a kind of family unity but they are used from the familiar "individual as the unit of illness" orientation and they refer more properly to the family as a cohesive group of individuals. We believe that the "family as a unit" concept is important in its own right, and that there is an advantage in clearly differentiating it from the familiar individual orientation.

1. *Family Patterns of Behavior.* Certain family characteristics began to come into view once it was possible to defocus the individual and to see "the family as a unit." Much of the writing about the project has been papers with brief descriptions of the most striking of these patterns. Among these patterns are the following:

2. *The Emotional Divorce.* In every family there was a marked emotional distance between the parents which we called the EMOTIONAL DIVORCE. Parents maintained this distance in different way. Some parents maintained the "divorce" with physical distance. When they were emotionally close, they fought and argued. Through physical distance, they were able to maintain an emotional distance and keep the conflict at a minimum. Other parents maintained a formal, polite, controlled distance. These marriages had the form and content of closeness, in that they went through the actions and used terms of endearment that gave an illusion of closeness, but the emotion of closeness was missing. Neither parent could communicate feelings and emotions to the other. Most of the parents maintained the "divorce" with varying communication of physical distance and controlled politeness.

a. *Overadequate-inadequate Reciprocity.* This is a term used to describe a constant pattern of parental functioning, present in all the families. Both parents are equally immature. In any given teamwork situation, one denies the immaturity and functions with a façade of overadequacy. The other denies the immaturity and functions with a façade of exaggerated inadequacy. The overadequacy of one functions in reciprocal relation to the inadequacy of the other. Neither can function in the mid-ground between the functioning position of great strength and the functioning position of weakness. Either can function in the over-adequate position and the other automatically finds self in the inadequate position. The one who makes a decision for the two of them automatically becomes the overadequate one who "dominates" the marriage, and the other sees self as "forced to submit." When the mother functions as the overadequate one, she is aggressive and dominating, while the father is weak and compliant. When the father functions as the overadequate one, he is cruel and authoritative, while the mother is shining and helpless. The intensity of the shifting reciprocity causes anxiety for both. They both use automatic mechanisms to stabilize the shifting and reduce the anxiety. In the effort to keep the closeness at a toned down distance, they develop individual spheres of activity that do not overlap, either or both may maintain important individual outside relationships, or they might use a third person to keep the emotional intensity out of their relationship.

The one who makes the decision that affects both, immediately becomes the "dominating" one. Decisions that are routine for other families, can become major crises. They avoid joint decisions. In critical situations, eiher parent may "take the bull by the horns" and assume the overadequate position, for brief or for extended periods. Over the years, the parents develop habitual patterns (the least anxious solution) for each situation. This leaves the impression of fixed personality characteristics and results in diagnostic appraisals like "the mother IS dominating." The diagnostic appraisals is inevitable with "the individual as the unit of illness" orientation. It was possible to see the change in these "fixed" states during the course of family psychotherapy.

b. *Intra-family Relationships.* Family members are quite different in their outside business and social relationships than they are in relation to each other. It is striking to see a father, who can function well as a leader in his business, become paralyzed by indecision within the family. Either parent can function "adequately" outside the family but, within the family, one becomes "inadequate." Family

members are quite different in individual psychotherapy relationships than they are in family psychotherapy. Each family member
has a different perception of the family. The family psychotherapist
has a view of the family that is different from any compilation of
individual viewpoints.

c. *The Interdependent Triad.* We have used this term to designate the
emotional interlocking between the father, the mother and the child
who becomes schizophrenic. In the family with a psychotic son or
daughter, these three people are involved in a special emotional
"oneness." The involvement may "spill over" and involve normal
siblings to a lesser extent, but the primary phenomenon is confined
to this central triad. In the beginning we believed that normal siblings were intimately involved but, as the families progressed in
psychotherapy, the normal siblings would separate themselves and
leave the father, mother and patient still locked in the emotional bind
of the "interdependent triad." From the time the mothers first knew
they were pregnant, the parents had a different kind of relationship
with this child, than with other children. This child came to fill the
functioning position as stabilizer of the "overadequate-inadequate
reciprocity." Clinically, the parents were separated by the emotional
divorce but either parents could have a close emotional relationship
with the child, if the other parent permitted. Descriptively, the child
appears to have served the function of an emotional stunt between
the parents, with the parents sharing the child, much as divorced
parents share their children.

d. *Growth Toward Maturity.* In the families that were able to resolve the
emotional divorce, and to grow toward maturity in family psychotherapy, there were observations that have far reaching implications
for mental health, for new theories concerning normal emotional
development, and for new principles concerning the rearing of children. When it was possible for the parents to resolve the emotional
divorce, and the parents could be more emotionally invested in each
other, than either was invested in the patient, then the patient began
automatically to grow toward maturity. When the parents would
lapse back to the emotional divorce, and either parent became more
invested in the patient than with the other parent, the patient would
automatically become more psychotic. The parents had all spent
years in reading and seeking advice about the proper way to raise
and handle the child. No matter what they tried, whether it be accep-
tance, firm kindness, giving love and attention, permissiveness, no
demands, realistic punishment, or whatever, the results were equally

unsuccessful. When the emotional divorce was resolved in family psychotherapy, it made little difference which approach they used in dealing with the patient. All approaches were equally successful.

The above patterns have been described in the literature in a few short paragraphs. Each pattern is important enough to deserve a full paper, or a chapter in a book. The patterns are intense and striking in disturbed families but they are also present to a lesser degree in "normal" families. We believe that the disturbed family with its exaggerated patterns and mechanisms, is not sufficiently recognized as a profitable avenue for the investigation of "normal" behavior. Once it is possible to see exaggerated patterns in a disturbed family (or individual), it is then possible to see the same pattern in a much less obvious form in the "normal."

3. *Family Psychotherapy.* Family psychotherapy was developed as a logical systematic therapeutic approach that emerged from the "family as a unit" concept. The family unit hypothesis was developed, point by point, from direct observation of the families, and the psychotherapy was designed, point by point, to deal therapeutically with the hypothesized configurations in the families. In this way the psychotherapy was an integral part of the research which utilized research findings, and contributed observational data back to the research. The psychotherapy was developed with a systematic set of principles based on the research hypothesis, a set of rules by which the therapy principles were structured into the clinical situation, and techniques used by the therapists in applying the rules. The family psychotherapy has become the most popular and copied part of the project. In the past 2 or 3 years, interest in family psychotherapy has spread rapidly. The staff did a paper on family psychotherapy at a national meeting in 1958. After the meeting, at least 20 therapists went home to try their own versions of family psychotherapy. The unique part of this family psychotherapy is that it was developed systematically from the theoretical hypothesis, while family psychotherapy practiced from an "individual as the unit of illness" orientation, is much more of an empirical "trial and error" procedure.

Family psychotherapy is quite different from individual or group psychotherapy. It is directed at analysis of existing intense relationships between family members rather than the "transferred" relationship between patient and analyst. In our experience, it provides an efficient therapeutic approach to a whole range of severe personality problems that ordinarily are inaccessible to, or that respond poorly to individual psychotherapy. For the neuroses, which ordinarily do respond to individual psychotherapy, family psychotherapy shows promise of becoming a quicker and more efficient method. An example was a recent experience (not an official part of the research) in which the presenting problem was a stomach ulcer in the husband. By treating husband and wife together, it was possible for both husband and wife to see the reciprocal mechanisms in the wife (the mirror image of the husband's psychological problem). An excellent therapeutic response was much easier and more rapid than the usual response of such a problem in individual psychotherapy.

4. *Development of a Family Theory of Schizophrenia.* A theory of schizophrenia, based on direct observations made from the "family unit" orientation and extensions of the "family unit" hypothesis has been developed. Briefly stated this theory evolved when the "family unit" orientation was applied to schizophrenia, and the theory has implications for all psychiatry and medicine. It is not suggested that this theory has a specific answer to the over-all understanding of schizophrenia or mental illness. It IS suggested that all existing theories of mental illness are based on the concept of "the individual as the unit of illness," that the theories all see the family through the eyes of the patient, and that "blaming" parents is inevitable with the individual orientation. We know from the family research that each individual sees the family in a different way, and that the "family unit" observations are on a completely different plane from any combination of individual viewpoints. It IS suggested that this family theory does offer a significant addition to previous theoretical thinking.

Present Status of the Research and Suggested Areas for More Detailed Study, Analysis and Writing

As the research now stands, only a fraction of its potential value has been realized. During the 4-year clinical operation, there were a few hundred interested visitors, many from foreign countries, who spent periods of an hour or two to several weeks sitting in on project meetings and making their own observations. Many returned home to incorporate some phase of the research into their own work. Since 1957, the staff has done 20 to 30 papers and informal presentations to national and local professional groups. During 1958 and early 1959, ten papers were accepted for publication. Three of these papers have appeared in print. The papers have been devoted largely to brief descriptions of large areas. An example was a recent paper in the American Journal of Psychiatry which described the project, described family relationship patterns, and touched on changes that occur in family psychotherapy, all in a 12-minute paper. There have been about 400 requests for reprints of that paper. To summarize, the professional communication about the research has been limited to brief general reports to a fraction of the potentially interested people. Some of the areas for special focus and study are:

1. *The Concept of "The Family as a Unit."* This appears first on each list. It belongs there. The family unit concept is crucial to the research. Among the people who have had detailed knowledge about the project, only a few have been able to shift from the "individual as the unit of illness" to the "family unit," or to maintain the family focus for long enough to look around. A goal is to communicate more clearly so that others may understand more easily.
2. *Family Psychotherapy.* This is the area with the most interest and appeal for the largest audience. Thus far, two papers have dealt with the family psychotherapy. This is the only family psychotherapy developed systematically from a theory. An adequate report on this work will make a sizeable contribution to the field.
3. *Family Relationship Patterns.* Existing papers have dealt with brief descriptions of the patterns listed on page 13 of this report. These need to be described in more detail with supporting observational data. The area of relationships between individual family members has not yet been touched for analysis or reporting. For instance, there is one prominent pattern in the mother-patient relationship. It is the situation in which the mother communicates one message on a verbal level, while on an action level she communicates the exact opposite. One ward observation will make this point clear. A mother was helping her adult schizophrenic son, who was eating. She buttered his bread, cut his meat, and poured his milk. At the very same time she was talking to him in calm mature language about growing up and learning to do things for himself. It has been helpful to us to think of an "action dialogue" which is in direct contradiction to the verbal language.
4. *Physical Illness and Somatic Reciprocation.* In the research families, it was a common phenomenon for one family member to develop a physical illness in response to anxiety in another. We have spoken of the way "the soma of one family member reciprocates with the psyche of another." These phenomena were clearest between two people whose chief emotional investment was in each other. One mother developed a severe physical illness within hours after each improvement in the psychotic daughter. The pattern is the same as that of the "overadequate-inadequate reciprocity' with the inadequacy expressed as physical illness. In these families, the most frequent manifestation of inadequacy was physical illness, the second was social and economic inadequacy, and the third was psychological. Among the physical inadequacies were

acute exacerbations of gall bladders, pelvic and prostatic conditions, acute flareup of chronic iritis, acute surgical problems, acute allergies and others. Among social and economic inadequacies were business failure, failure in school, anti-social behavior and delinquency. The most frequent psychological inadequacy (other than psychosis in the patient) was depression and overt anxiety states. Almost every family had at least one major surgical operation during the study. A frequent pattern in the "interdependent triad" was (1) patient shift from relative adequacy to inadequacy (psychosis more severe). (2) Mother, in functioning reciprocity to patient, shift to greater adequacy (more efficient, decisive and stronger). (3) Father in functioning reciprocity to overadequate mother, shift to less adequacy (get sick, depressed or do poorly in business—two fathers went bankrupt in the year after the patient became psychotic). A constant characteristic of the family reciprocation is that each family member explains changes as related to factors outside the family or inside his own body. Family members focus entirely on the fact that each is a unique independent being. They resist the notion that changes in one's self might be related to the functioning of another. This area contains consistent repeating clinical facts to support the "family as a unit" hypothesis. Very little work has been done in analyzing the data for presenting these striking observations.

7

Seminal Contributions of
Bowen's NIMH Family Study Project

INTRODUCTION

There were many significant findings from Bowen's NIMH Family Study Project. This section is an effort to summarize some of the seminal contributions of the project. Several of these will be reviewed.

A Long-Term Study of Families Is Possible

A theory based four-year study and observation of hospitalized families with a schizophrenic child was successfully completed. It was possible for families to live on an inpatient research unit for long periods of time. The average length of stay was about a year. In addition, outpatient families with similar clinical symptoms to the inpatient families were evaluated and treated which offered a comparison group with less intense problems.

Family Patterns Identified

During the Family Research Project definite family patterns were identified and defined. Among these were reciprocity, the emotional divorce, and over- and under-functioning. In addition, one of the project psychiatrists was the primary care physician for all family members. A strong relationship was observed between emotional and physical symptoms.

The Main Finding

The main finding of the Family Study Project was the concept of the family as an emotional unit. It means that symptoms in one person reflect emotional processes involving the entire family. This concept is a significantly different way of thinking about individual symptoms and has important implications for theory and practice today.

Family Psychotherapy Developed

Family psychotherapy, which emerged from the concept of the family as an emotional unit, is a different way to work clinically with families. This method is distinctly different from traditional individual, family or group therapy. It requires the therapeutic abilities of thinking in terms of a family unit, and relating and treating the family as a unit.

A New Therapeutic Role Emerged

The family psychotherapist's purpose is the analysis of intra-family relationships based on particular theoretical concepts. Family psychotherapy fundamentally alters the nature of the therapeutic alliance. It is critical to relate to the family unit and manage over-involvement with any one person. The family psychotherapist does not attempt to psychologically replace a parent, enhance a therapeutic alliance, or join the family. In addition, the emotionality surrounding the problem is left within the original family relationship. A method of treatment originally developed for the family unit, now has applications in working with couples and individuals. Family psychotherapy embraces a unique type of therapeutic relationship compared to other treatment modalities. Later, Bowen actually preferred the term "coaching" to more accurately describe his method of working with people.

NOTE

This focus on seminal contributions was suggested by my former AAMFT supervisor, Leon T. Webber, D.MN., during a luncheon at his home in Anchorage, AK, in the summer of 2010. —Jack Butler

8

Family Psychotherapy: A Summary

Family psychotherapy began during the four-year Family Research Project at NIMH from 1954 to 1958. During the first year mothers and their (diagnosed as) schizophrenic daughters were hospitalized on a special research unit. In the first year of the project Bowen and his colleagues experienced firsthand the challenges of working intensively with these families. The intensities of the mother-daughter dyads affected the staff, were substantial and unexpected, and actually threatened the project's existence.

In the later part of the first year of the project, a landmark discovery was made. The problems of the mother-daughter dyads were not limited to them; the entire nuclear family was involved. The severe symptoms in the child came to be viewed as an emotional process involving all members of the family, not just the mothers and daughters. This finding was termed the "family as an emotional unit" hypothesis, and became one cornerstone of the Family Research Project. As a result, for the last three years of the project, only entire families with a child diagnosed as schizophrenic were admitted.

The treatment of the family unit was derived from the concept of the family as an emotional unit. Daily meetings involving both staff and families were undertaken for the last three years of the project, and replaced individual psychoanalytic psychotherapy for all family members. It was these daily staff-patient groups that were later termed family psychotherapy. The therapeutic focus was on the treatment of the family as an emotional unit rather than establishing and interpreting a traditional patient-therapist relationship.

Family psychotherapy, initiated as a method to work clinically with project families, was derived from a theoretical concept. This method was also used with outpatient families who were found to display similar but less intense family patterns than the inpatient families. Daily family psychotherapy was found to have positive benefits. First, the overall level of family and staff tension was reduced and second, the level of staff over-involvement with family members could be clearly seen and effectively managed.

Working with family units required the ability to emotionally and clinically relate to the family. The intellectual understanding of the concept of the family as an emotional unit was straightforward. However, it was more challenging to put this concept into operation, to shift from a predominately individual orientation and work to manage emotional over-identification with individuals.

References

Ackerman, N. (1937). The Family as a Social and Emotional Unit. In D. Block & R. Simon (Eds.), *The Strength of Family Therapy: Selected Papers of Nathan W. Ackerman* (pp. 153–158). New York: Brunner/Mazel, Inc.

Basamania, B. (1961). The Family As a Unit of Study and Treatment Workshop. 1959. Paper No. 4. The Emotional Life of the Family: Inferences For Social Casework. *American Journal of Orthopsychiatry, 31,* 74–86.

Bowen, M. (1954). Analysis of NIH Program Activities. Project Description Sheet. *Influence of the Early Mother-Child Relationship in the Later Development of Schizophrenia.* (December). L. Murray Bowen Papers. (Accession 2006-003, Box 4, NIMH Annual Reports, 1954–1958. History of Medicine Division, National Library of Medicine, Bethesda, Maryland).

Bowen, M. (1955a). *Interim Report on Research Project. Influence of the early mother-child relationship in the development of schizophrenia.* (May). L. Murray Bowen Papers. (Accession 2006-003, Box 4, NIMH Annual Reports, 1954–1958. History of Medicine Division, National Library of Medicine, Bethesda, Maryland).

Bowen, M. (1955b). *Analysis of NIH Program Activities. Project Description Sheet. Influence of the early mother-child relationship in the development of schizophrenia.* (December). L. Murray Bowen Papers. (Accession 2006-003, Box 4, NIMH Annual Reports, 1954–1958. History of Medicine Division, National Library of Medicine, Bethesda, Maryland).

Bowen, M. (1956a). *Individual Project Report. Study and Treatment of Schizophrenia as a Family Problem.* L. Murray Bowen Papers. (Accession 2006-003, Box 4, NIMH Annual Report. History of Medicine Division, National Library of Medicine, Bethesda, Maryland).

Bowen, M. (1956b). *The Family Project.* L. Murray Bowen Papers. (Accession 2006-003, Box 6, The Family Project. History of Medicine Division, National Library of Medicine, Bethesda, Maryland).

Bowen, M. (1956c). *Formulation of 3 East Family Study Project, July 16, 1956. The Treatment of Schizophrenia Using Modifications of Psychoanalytic Techniques & Extensions of Psychoanalytic theory.* L. Murray Bowen Papers. (Accession 2006-003, Box 2, NIMH Research Reports. History of Medicine Division, National Library of Medicine, Bethesda, Maryland).

Bowen, M., Dysinger, R., Brodey, W., & Basamania, B. (1957). *The Development of Techniques of Dealing With Five Family Units and Some Patterns Observed in the Transaction of Those Families.* L. Murray Bowen Papers. (Accession 2006-003, Box 3, Articles with handwritten notes. History of Medicine Division, National Library of Medicine, Bethesda, Maryland).

Bowen, M. (1957). *Individual Project Report for Calendar Year 1957. Study and Treatment of Schizophrenia as a Family Problem.* L. Murray Bowen Papers. (Accession 2006-003, Box 4, 3E Project. History of Medicine Division, National Library of Medicine, Bethesda, Maryland).

Bowen, M. (1958). *Psychotherapy of the Family as a Unit.* Unpublished manuscript. L. Murray Bowen Papers. (Accession 2006-003, Box 2, American Orthopsychiatry Presentation. History of Medicine Division, National Library of Medicine, Bethesda, Maryland).

Bowen, M. (1959). *Family Research Project for The Study and Treatment of Schizophrenic Patients and Their Families.* Unpublished manuscript. L. Murray Bowen Papers. (Accession 2006-003, Box 6, Formulation of Family Study Project. History of Medicine Division, National Library of Medicine, Bethesda, Maryland).

Bowen, M. (1961). The Family As The Unit of Study and Treatment Workshop, 1959. Paper No. 1. Family Psychotherapy. *American Journal of Orthopsychiatry, 31*, 40–60.

Bowen, M. (1978). *Family Therapy in Clinical Practice.* Lanham, Maryland: Rowman & Littlefield.

Boyd, C. (Ed.). (2008). *Commitment to Principles: The Letters of Murray Bowen, M.D.* (Available from Clarence Boyd, Escondido Farm Family Center, 2824 Escondido Farm Road, Garner, N.C., 27529.)

Brodey, W. (1961). The Family As The Unit of Study and Treatment Workshop, 1959. Paper No. 3. Image, Object and Narcissistic Relationships. *American Journal of Orthopsychiatry, 31*, 69–73.

Dysinger, R. (1961). The Family As The Unit of Study and Treatment Workshop, 1959. Paper No. 2. A Family Perspective of the Diagnosis on Individual Members. *American Journal of Orthopsychiatry, 31*, 61–68.

Guerin, P. J. (1972). Family Therapy: The First Twenty-Five Years. In P. J. Guerin (Ed.), *Family Therapy Theory and Practice,* (pp. 2–22). New York: Garner Press.

Kerr, M. E. and Bowen, M. (1988). *Family Evaluation.* New York: Norton Press.

Index

About the Contributors

Murray Bowen, M.D. (1913–1990) received his medical education from the University of Tennessee Medical School in 1937. His psychiatric training was at the Menninger Foundation in Topeka, Kansas beginning in 1946. He remained at Menninger's in training and as a staff member until 1954 when he began his historic family research project at the NIMH in Bethesda, Maryland. In 1959, he became a faculty member in the Department of Psychiatry at Georgetown University Medical School. He founded the Georgetown Family Center in 1975 and was its director until his death in 1990. His book, *Family Therapy in Clinical Practice*, has become a classic in the field and contains many of his important published papers. He was a life fellow of the American Psychiatric Association. Dr. Bowen's unpublished papers, videotapes, and other materials are now housed in the History of Medicine Division of the National Library of Medicine.

John F. Butler, Ph.D., maintains a private practice at Rose Street Mental Health Care in Wichita Falls, TX. He is a licensed clinical social worker, marriage & family therapist, and an AAMFT Clinical Member and Approved Supervisor. He received his M.S.W. from the University of Michigan-Ann Arbor, and his Ph.D. in Social Welfare from the University of Wisconsin-Madison. He retired as a Colonel from the United States Air Force in 1999. He was the Associate Chief of Clinical Social Work for the Air Force Surgeon General while at Andrews AFB, Maryland. Dr. Butler trained at the Georgetown Family Center (now the Bowen Center for the Study of the Family) for five years. He received the Caskie Research Award from the Bowen Center in 2010 for his work on the Bowen Archives at the NIMH.

Joanne Bowen, Ph.D., received her M.A. and Ph.D. from Brown University in 1990 and is currently Curator of Zooarchaeology, Collections, Conservations, and Museums at the Colonial Williamsburg Foundation, Williamsburg, Virginia. In addition, she is a Research Professor, Department of Anthropology, College of William and Mary, in Williamsburg. She is President and Executive Director, of the Board for Leaders for Tomorrow, a not-for-profit organization established to preserve Murray Bowen's archives held at the National Library of Medicine in Bethesda, Maryland.

Michael E. Kerr, M.D., is the Emeritus Director of the Bowen Center for the Study of the Family. He and his wife Kathy now reside in Islesboro, Maine. He and Dr. Bowen separately authored the classic book *Family Evaluation* in 1988. Dr. Kerr continues to lecture and teach at the Bowen Center, and travels widely in the United States, Australia, and the Far-East presenting on Bowen theory and its applications.